JEFF S

MW00681243

straight talk about

SPIRITUAL
WARFARE

WHAT THE BIBLE TEACHES
WHAT YOU NEED TO KNOW

CRC Publications
Grand Rapids, Michigan

Straight Talk About Spiritual Warfare: What the Bible Teaches, What You Need to Know. © 1999 by CRC Publications, 2850 Kalamazoo Ave. SE, Grand Rapids, Michigan 49560. We welcome your comments. Call us at 1-800-333-8300 or e-mail us at editors@crcpublications.org.

Library of Congress Cataloging-in-Publication Data
Stam, Jeff, 1950-
    Straight talk about spiritual warfare: what the Bible teaches, what you need to know / Jeff Stam.
       p.   cm.
    Includes bibliographical references.
    ISBN 1-56212-413-7
    · 1. Spiritual warfare—Biblical teaching. I. Title.
BS680.S73S73   1999
235'.4—dc21   99-31064
                                             CIP

10 9 8 7 6 5 4 3 2 1

I dedicate this book to all who have allowed my wife, Denise, and me to be part of their journey to spiritual victory. You have honored us with your trust. It is our prayer that you will always stand firm in knowing Christ and the power of his resurrection (Phil. 3:10). Hold high his word of truth and wield well the sword of the Spirit.

CONTENTS

PREFACE

In my early years of ministry a deeply troubled young lady was referred to me. I gave her some simple psychological tests, but she wasn't able to answer the questions in a rational way even though she was a college graduate. She had trouble reconstructing the last five years of her life, which included several hospitalizations in the psych ward.

Even though I was getting nowhere with her, I agreed to meet with her again, but only if she would come under the authority of our church. Suddenly her whole demeanor changed, and with a different voice she said, "I've got to get out of here." It didn't require a lot of discernment to know that I was facing a spiritual battle. As she started to leave I said, "Judy, is Jesus your Lord?" She turned around with clenched teeth and said, "You ask Jesus who my Lord is." Then she left the room.

I followed her down a flight of stairs and repeated the question. She suddenly stopped and said yes. After returning to my office I said, "Judy, there is a battle going on for your mind. Has anybody ever talked to you about it?"

No, she said. Either they didn't know or they were afraid. But she knew!

I didn't have a clue about how to help her. Seminary had not prepared me to counsel such people, much less understand the truth that "our struggle is not against flesh and blood, but against the rulers, against the authorities, against the powers of this dark world and against the spiritual forces of evil in the heavenly realms" (Eph. 6:12). With a great deal of prayer, soul searching, and truth from God's Word, after several months I was able to see her gain some victories.

Several other experiences as a pastor led me to start a class on spiritual conflicts and counseling at Talbot School of Theology, where the Lord had called me to teach. I started the class because I wanted to know what God had to say about who we are, who our enemy is, and how we are to engage him. At first it was as if I were a first grader teaching two-year-olds. What I didn't know was profound. But every year the class grew—from 18 students to 23, then 35, then 65, 150, and finally 250 students signed up for a Masters of Theology elective!

I came to realize that Jesus is the wonderful counselor and the One who delivers us from the powers of darkness. Our role as pastors, counselors, and encouragers is that of a facilitator. Eventually I learned how to help people resolve their personal and spiritual conflicts in a quiet and controlled way. I have seen the ineffectiveness of polarizing into psychotherapeutic ministries that ignore the reality of the spiritual world or deliverance ministries that ignore personal responsibility and developmental issues. We have a whole God who deals with the whole person. To be effective in ministry we must take into account all of reality and hold each person accountable for his or her own attitudes and actions. This kind of thinking led me away from confrontational power encounters that assumed I had to pray for others or somehow "fix" them.

Our battle is better understood as a truth encounter, because it is truth that sets people free. This book is about the truth that sets people free. I first met Jeff while teaching a Doctor of Ministry class at Trinity Evangelical Divinity School. I have seen him grow in knowledge and experience. He knows how to help people resolve their personal and spiritual conflicts. This biblically-based book will help you understand the spiritual world we are living in and how we can live victoriously in Christ. Christ is the answer and his truth will set you free. Jesus is the bondage breaker.

Dr. Neil T. Anderson
Founder and President of Freedom in Christ Ministries

INTRODUCTION

"Pastor, I need your help for a serious problem I have."

"Alright, Benjamin, what is it?"

"Well, it's this way. After I go to bed at night and fall asleep, I start traveling to other places. I know this is bad, but I don't know what to do about it. I can't stop it."

"Benjamin, are you sure you are not just dreaming?"

"No, I know this is real. And it has not happened just once or twice, but many times."

"Okay, Benjamin. Tonight I will sleep in your hut on my trekbed and I will watch to see what happens. If you're dreaming, I'll wake you up. If you start moving, I will grab you and not let you go. Then, in the morning we will together review what actually happened."

Benjamin turned around in disgust. "Pastor, there is nothing to see or hold on to. It is my spirit that is traveling, not the body. My body will stay in bed."

With those words Benjamin left me, appalled at my attitude and my ignorance. Here was a rather common problem and I, a white educated pastor, did not understand what was going on. Clearly I had not been of any help to him.

This story was related by Jan Boer, a Christian Reformed World Missions missionary to Nigeria for almost thirty years ("Opening the Reformed World to the Powers," *Perspectives,* February, 1994, p. 16). It clearly illustrates the challenge that Western-educated Christians face in approaching the topic of spiritual warfare on the personal level. We have been trained to think about life and its events in a rational, scientific, empirical, no-nonsense manner. Even for those of us raised in Christian homes, educated in Christian schools, and catechized in solid, Christian churches, stepping outside this rational paradigm can be disconcerting. It was for me, and it has been for many others.

However, if we are willing to believe something for no other reason than full trust in the source, that which makes us uncomfortable now can become bearable, and—with time—perhaps even comfortable. The gift of believing the Bible just because it is the Bible, of not allowing God to be boxed into any preconceived limitations of measurement or experience, of not having to "explain" everything, does wonders for the level of expectation we have in God and God's promises. The daily Christian walk can be exhilarating, even in the valleys filled with shadows. Victory can be a present reality, not just a pie-in-the-sky hope for another existence. This is spiritual warfare, as God meant it to be fought and won.

Obviously we need to read and apply God's Word in the context of careful study and appropriate methods of interpretation. Likewise, we must be theologically prudent when we approach the topic of spiritual warfare. However, it is possible to be so cautious that we never get around to the topic at all! That's what happened to me as I chased elusive theological answers to a plethora of questions. Gradually I saw that I had merely exchanged the paradigm of scientific rationalism for one of theological temperance. As I sought to build an airtight theological defense, I would be hit hard on both flanks with more questions: How do you account for gifts of discernment and visions? What about memories and back-to-the womb experiences? What about the possibility of MPD (Multiple Personality Disorder)? What about territorial spirits? The questions were legion.

No, I do not have the answers to all these questions and I cannot point you to a single source that does. Indeed, the Bible has all the principles we need, but we still must do the work of understanding them. Then, with much prayer for wisdom and guidance, we must apply biblical truth to spiritual warfare as it takes place in our personal lives, in Christ's Body, and in God's world.

Why This Book?

Numerous resources are already available on the topic of spiritual warfare, so why write another book? Mainly because my Reformed tradition hasn't done much with this topic. That's not because people in our churches are not affected or interested (we have addressed some related topics). I'm convinced our neglect is due to our need to tie up all the theological "loose ends." Perhaps we need to remind ourselves that dealing with the reality of Satan and his powers was so central in Reformational thinking that it became the major theme of the Reformation's "fight song." While the account of Martin Luther throwing his inkwell at Satan may or may not be apocryphal, his penning of *A Mighty Fortress* certainly is not:

> A mighty fortress is our God, a bulwark never failing;
> our helper he, amid the flood of mortal ills prevailing.
> *For still our ancient foe does seek to work us woe;*
> *his craft and power are great, and armed with cruel hate,*
> *on earth is not his equal.*
>
> *Did we in our own strength confide, our striving would be losing,*
> *were not the right Man on our side, the Man of God's own choosing.*
> *You ask who that may be, Christ Jesus, it is he;*

Lord Sabaoth his name, from age to age the same;
and he must win the battle.

And though this world with devils filled, should threaten to undo us,
we will not fear, for God has willed his truth to triumph through us.
The prince of darkness grim, we tremble not for him;
his rage we can endure, for lo! his doom is sure;
one little word shall fell him.

That Word *above all earthly powers, no thanks to them* abideth;
the Spirit and the gifts are ours through him who with us sideth.
Let goods and kindred go, this mortal life also;
the body they may kill: God's truth abideth still;
his kingdom is forever! (italics mine)

The main goal of this book is to provide an easy-to-read introduction to the subject of spiritual warfare. I hope it will be useful for individual reflection and for small group study and discussion. You'll find questions at the end of each section; use them as springboards for your personal wrestling with the material, or, if you are studying the material as part of a small group, as fodder for further discussion. Many of the questions are designed to help you or your group search out a biblical perspective. I've written a separate leader's guide for leaders of small groups.

Whether you study this book with a small group or read it on your own, I hope it will serve as a first step toward understanding the personal battle about which the apostle Paul warns and in which Christians find themselves enmeshed. You'll find a number of suggestions for follow-up study in the annotated bibliography at the end of this book (not all of the available resources on spiritual warfare represent solid, biblical reflection, but some do).

A Down-to-Earth Approach

In writing this book and its leader's guide, I've attempted to bring balance to the topic, to rein it in, if you will, so that it can be approached openly and wisely, with respect but without undue fear. While I can't answer every question, I trust that this book will bring more people together to honestly seek out those answers (and to have the wisdom and trust to accept the fact that some questions have no answers).

Writing style, even on a research level, has changed in the past twenty years. In the late '70s when I presented a draft of my graduate thesis, I was advised that the style was too "homey," that I needed to make it sound more "scholarly." Translated, this meant "Make the sentences more difficult to understand and use a ten-dollar vocabulary." Ten years later, when presenting my post-graduate dissertation, I was (thankfully) advised to "Make it simple. Keep sentences short. Use vocabulary that is precise, yet readable." I've tried to follow that advice here. Still, I wish this project could be interactive. I want to speak *with* you of these matters, not lecture *at* you.

The material has evolved from a seminar entitled *The Battle of the Angels*. I've had the privilege of presenting this seminar to young people and adults, to laypeople and to clergy. The seminar, as does this book, revolves around four rhetorical questions, a satisfactory and positive answer to each allowing us to proceed to the next. Those questions are:

- Do Satan and demons exist, and are they active in the world today?

- Can Satan or demons attack Christians?

- Should the church involve itself in spiritual warfare?

- How?

These four questions represent the four divisions of the book.

Organization of This Book

Part 1: Do Satan and demons exist, and are they active in the world today?

In this section, which is primarily a discussion of worldview, I've included my personal story as it relates to spiritual warfare and, for lack of a better term, deliverance or "freedom" ministry. I experienced a significant gap between my *believing* in God and my *practicing* the reality of the spiritual, especially in the realm of the "supernatural." I suspect it's a gap that others have also experienced. It's surprising how readily we profess belief in God but automatically balk at all things "out of the ordinary."

In this first section we'll look at two extremes: animism, which is clearly understood by the majority of the Third World (or the "two-thirds world," as some prefer), and the Western worldview. The balance between these extremes is found in a biblical worldview, one that recognizes the reality of the supernatural, the spiritual, and its interaction with daily life.

Section 2: Can Satan or demons attack Christians?

In this section we will first make sure we are on the same page when we talk about who and what a Christian is. Then we'll briefly turn our attention to correct vocabulary (the proper and improper use of the word *possession*). It's easy to lose balance at this point, finding demons behind every bush and blaming them for every sin and aberration. That's why it's important to consider other enemies, namely our fleshly nature and the world, and how Satan works in conjunction with them. And we'll ask why Satan would want to attack us in the first place.

It's been said that Satan is like a mad dog, but he is on a leash. In this section of the book we'll examine that leash. How long is it? How strong is it? Finally, we will briefly (but carefully, because we begin to enter areas of speculation) identify various degrees of demonization and how they can be treated.

Section 3: Should the church involve itself in spiritual warfare?

If Satan and demons do exist and are active in the world today, and if they can, at least to some extent, demonize a believer, should the church become actively involved in spiritual warfare? Perhaps the answer to that question seems obvious, yet some would say "No way." Here we take a look at some of the risks of the church being involved—or not being involved—in spiritual warfare. Peter warns us that the devil is like a roaring lion, on the prowl for someone to devour (1 Pet. 5:8). Jesus warns his disciples (and presumably us) that Satan has actually presented a request to God's throne to sift us. There are reasons to be cautious. But we also need to ask if caution in battle means retreat or, as this book will argue, wise, strategic offense and defense.

Section 4: How?

If we are to enter into this spiritual fray that is not of flesh and blood, that is fought on an unfamiliar battlefield, that uses weapons with which we are often unfamiliar, that is fought against an astute, invisible, treacherous enemy—how should the church respond? Even if we are willing to be obedient, even if we are willing to muster all the faith we can, even if we are willing to take extraordinary risks, how do we go about waging spiritual war?

In answering the questions of the first three sections, I depend significantly on Dr. Timothy Warner, formerly dean of the School of World Missions at Trinity Evangelical Divinity School and now on staff with Freedom in Christ of La Habra, California. In answering the *how* question, I've leaned very heavily on a process that Dr. Neil Anderson describes as "truth encounter" in his bestselling books *Victory Over the Darkness* and *The Bondage Breaker*. I owe much to both men for stretching my own worldview and for helping me find balance in the treatment of this topic.

This section will look at the pros and cons of several methodologies; however, the decision about which to choose will be left to you, the reader. It is my desire to introduce you to the reality of spiritual warfare, to provide some balance, to eliminate some fears, and to point you to reliable sources for further study.

A Holistic Ministry

Finally, I would be negligent if I addressed only the spiritual side of spiritual warfare. While I make no attempt to present an in-depth psychological or physiological analysis of the issues and symptoms that sometime accompany or, at times, mimic spiritual oppression, it is of utmost importance that we minister to individuals holistically. We cannot ignore our bodies and our minds, and the fact that they, along with our spiritual being, define who we are. We should not treat chemical imbalance or severe emotional trauma as only a spiritual problem. Nor should we ignore the potential effect that trauma can have on our spiritual well-being or the types of footholds or openings that it can give to spiritual oppression.

Appendix C is the edited transcript of a roundtable discussion by several medical, mental health care, and clerical professionals who give us their perspective on spiritual warfare. All have seriously sought to find the appropriate balance that allows for the practice of a fully biblical worldview, while acknowledging the importance and validity of mental health, medical, and spiritual care.

God the Father and Jesus the Son have given us a multitude of wonderful promises throughout Scripture. For most of us, specific promises take on meaning and become more precious in direct proportion to a specific need or period of trial in our lives. As we enter into a study of spiritual warfare, of enemies not of flesh and blood, and of roaring lions, let us remember the promise that God gives for the hour of need: "The one that is in you is greater than the one that is in the world" (1 John 4:4). To God be the glory!

REFLECTION ON THE INTRODUCTION

This section is intended for individual reflection and/or group discussion.

Bible Study

Read 2 Kings 6:8-23

1. What did Elisha's servant see, and what was his immediate reaction (v. 15)? How would you have reacted?

2. Elisha tries to calm his servant by explaining that there wasn't a problem, that "we outnumber them" (v. 16). Do you think the servant was comforted much by Elisha's statement? Why or why not? Can you think of a time when you were in a crisis situation and someone tried to give you spiritual assurance that wasn't helpful?

3. Assuming that Elisha's servant traveled with him, he must have witnessed a number of miraculous events and God's hand at work, including the episode of the floating axhead recounted earlier in the chapter. Why wasn't the servant more expectant? Why did he panic so easily? Can you think of times when this has happened to you, even though you had plenty of evidence of God's hand at work? Why do you suppose this happens?

4. What did Elisha ask God to do for his servant, and what was the result (v. 17)? Has something similar ever happened to you?

5. Can you think of a New Testament example of someone who witnessed the miraculous, knew all the correct theological answers, but still had trouble grasping spiritual reality?

General Discussion

1. What is the first thing that the term "spiritual warfare" brings to your mind? Are you comfortable with the topic or do you have some reservations about it?

2. The four sections of the book are divided by four rhetorical questions:
   - Do Satan and demons exist, and are they active in the world today?
   - Can Satan or demons attack Christians?
   - Should the church involve itself in spiritual warfare?
   - How?
   What is your immediate "yes" or "no" answer to the first three questions?

A Reading

For I am convinced that neither death nor life, neither angels nor demons, neither the present nor the future, nor any powers, neither height nor depth, nor anything else in all creation, will be able to separate us from the love of God that is in Christ Jesus our Lord.

—Romans 8:38-39

QUESTION 1

Do Satan and demons exist, and are they active in the world today?

The Demonic Boy at the Foot of Mount Tabor

—James J. Tissot, 1836-1902

CHAPTER 1

THE HYPNOTIST

It all began with a hypnotist. Technically, I suppose that's incorrect, since the shaping and reshaping of my thinking had been occurring for years. At times that reshaping was rather drastic, seriously challenging prior notions about how God works or doesn't work in our lives and our world. However, I had never thought about those adjustments, that tweaking that God was doing to my thought-filtering system, in terms of something called a "worldview." I had no idea that the major paradigm by which I interpreted reality was going to be radically tested. But I'm getting ahead of my story. Let me go back to the hypnotist.

We were on home-service in Michigan, back from Central America for the summer, and had the opportunity to attend the twentieth reunion of my wife's high school class. The entertainer was a well-known hypnotist. This individual was a professional with more than twenty years of experience and a solid reputation in his field. He often helped the local law enforcement units with difficult cases. As we were waiting for the program to begin, the woman sitting next to me leaned over and asked, "Do you think this is okay?" I could tell that what she was really asking was, "Should Christians be doing or participating in this? Is this something mystical or spiritual that God would not approve of?" Warning bells reminding me of earlier challenges to my preconceived notions should have been ringing; but I dismissed her question with something like, "I wouldn't worry about it; it's just a question of mind over matter, purely psychological." She obviously wasn't convinced, but she didn't press the point with me.

The hypnotist asked for audience participation and volunteers. He apparently planned to entertain us by getting people to quack and bark and generally embarrass themselves. A few volunteered, but the hypnotist couldn't get to first base with them. He asked for other volunteers, suggesting that the originals weren't relaxing and letting go. Still no success. Then he tried some group suggestion. Nothing. At this point he hinted that his subjects weren't cooperating. Later he suggested that the whole audience wasn't cooperating. After more frustration, growing tension, and not a single "quack" or "woof," he finally pulled a check out of his coat pocket (his payment for the evening). He gave it back to the emcee and left the auditorium declaring that nothing like that had ever happened to him before.

As people filed out of the auditorium, the evening's entertainment cut short, little groups quickly formed in the hallway to chat about how "interesting" the hypnotist's failure was. At that point the woman who had been seated next to me quietly mentioned, "I prayed that if this wasn't of God that God would not allow it to work." I didn't respond, but did find myself following Mary's example and "guarding these things in my heart."

That was Saturday evening. On Monday morning I was off to Chicago to take a course as part of a post-graduate program at Trinity Evangelical Divinity School in Deerfield, Illinois. The course, entitled "Power Encounter," was taught by Dr. Timothy Warner, then director of Trinity's School of World Missions. I had been attracted to the course simply because it sounded interesting and because I thought it might be similar to a very popular course on signs and wonders that had been offered at Fuller Theological Seminary in California. My mind was not closed to the possibility of what we have come to call the "extraordinary," but I did maintain a "prove it" attitude, not wanting to be anybody's fool.

I mention this because people who know of my work assume that I was first introduced to the subject of this book as part of my Third World missionary experience. That is not the case. My introduction and initial exposure to spiritual warfare happened right in the middle of Bible-belt evangelical America. In that course at Trinity my comfort zone was stretched and my theological assumptions were challenged. Try as I might, I could not find any blatant errors in Dr. Warner's position. Clearly, other interpretations were possible, but when challenged to accept biblical text for what it seemed to say without the filter of "having to explain away all the extraordinary, outside-my-realm-of-experience stuff," I found it difficult indeed to deny the plausibility of present-day spiritual warfare on the personal level. Putting it bluntly, I found that I just might have to take Paul's warning in Ephesians 6:10-12 literally and seriously.

As I drove home at the end of the week, I was reeling. I couldn't explain away the testimonials and videos that we, as a class, had heard and seen. If I believed that these people were simply deluded or, worse yet, lying to me and doctoring evidence, that in itself created a greater crisis of faith than did believing what they said. More disturbing was the fact that even though I'd been a Christian for many years and, I felt, a growing and maturing missionary pastor, I did not approach life with a fully integrated biblical worldview. I realized in that drive to Michigan that I had two options. I could merely turn in the required assignments to complete the course and file it all away in my "interesting, but do-not-open drawer," or I could follow up on this matter and risk turning my whole ministry upside down.

I decided to remain passive. A few weeks later, my responsibilities as field director made it necessary to visit Honduras for interviews with our missionary families there. Since they all knew that I'd been in the States studying, it was natural for them to ask about it. During those visits all the missionaries I spoke with, with one exception, shared with me something that had happened at some point in their ministry career that they felt was directly influenced by demonic or satanic involvement. Even more interesting to me was the fact all but one of those missionaries had never shared their story with other ministry colleagues.

Once word got out that the field director was "open" to talking about these things, missionaries began sharing more stories, nationals shared experiences they had previously felt North American missionaries wouldn't begin to understand, and we started to see things from a totally different perspective. Some of our national pastors were obviously thinking that it was about time the missionaries "woke up and smelled the coffee." For me, it was like suddenly putting on a new pair of glasses. I began seeing things differently. People started telling me about bondage to fears, poltergeist-type experiences, night terrors, demonic attacks, experiences with *culanderos* (spiritual healers) and witches, and dabbling in magic.

I soon found it was easy to lose balance, to see a demon under every rock or behind every bush. More than half a century ago, C. S. Lewis recognized this pitfall and creatively warned us about it in the oft-quoted *Screwtape Letters*:

> There are two equal and opposite extremes into which our race can fall about the devils. One is to disbelieve in their existence. The other is to believe, and to feel an excessive and unhealthy interest in them. They themselves are equally pleased by both errors and hail a materialist [non believer] or a magician [extremist] with the same delight.

While I have no desire to make this book a collection of stories of the wild and weird, allow me to share an event that established two important things for me and some of my ministry coworkers: the reality of spiritual warfare in the form of overt, demonic manifestation and attack; and the need for further training and balance in this area.

Oscar, a young man in his early twenties, arrived a little early for the evening service at Los Guidos (Costa Rica). Oscar was not a regular, but apparently had attended a few times, offering to play his guitar. As this was not the church I regularly attended, nor for which I had any supervisory responsibility, I had never met this young man.

Upon arrival, Oscar immediately went to the front of the church, raised his hands, and began "praising" God. As the pastor began the service, Oscar continued his loud praise. While I was used to having Pentecostal believers visit our churches and praise God in this style, I felt uncomfortable. I rose from my place in the back pew and made my way forward, intending to ask this young man to please allow the pastor to lead the service without interruption. On the way up, I quickly whispered to a fellow missionary to pray.

"What are you going to do?" he asked.

"I don't know, just pray," I answered. Obviously I was feeling more disquieted about this than I realized. I gently placed my hand on Oscar's shoulder so as to get his attention, and immediately he fell to the floor and began convulsing and shouting. My missionary colleague ran up beside me and demanded, "What did you do?" to which I replied, "I didn't do anything."

I felt we had a demonic manifestation on our hands. I had seen manifestations on a few occasions, but they were either on video or in a "controlled" deliverance session. We brought Oscar to the pastor's house, which was attached to the church, and tried to gain control of the situation. I asked the name of the spirit that was manifesting itself (something I remembered from my reading). The answer was "Oscar." I asked again, and the answer was the same. Then I remembered that demons cannot declare the lordship of Jesus Christ. So we asked Oscar: "Who is Lord?" Twice he replied, "Jesus."

By this time I was confused and had exhausted my limited knowledge about demons. Still convinced that we were dealing with a spirit (I attribute that conviction to a momentary gift of discernment), I commanded in the name of Jesus that whoever or whatever was speaking through the mouth of Oscar identify itself. At that point his face contorted as he stated, "Beelzebú" (Spanish equivalent of Beelzebub, later identified as a spirit of false religiosity).

Then "Oscar" started acting like a wild ninja, tearing furniture apart, coming at us with boards with nails protruding from them, and karate-kicking through one-and-a-half inch thick, solid cement walls. During the next hour or so, seven spirits identified themselves and we believed that three or four left, but we did not feel very victorious. Eventually the pastor came over (the racket was disrupting his attempts to lead the service). We asked him to go back and have the congregation keep singing. That seemed to quiet "Oscar" down enough for him to peacefully depart.

I went home bruised and shaken and thinking to myself, "This doesn't feel like victory." Obviously, I had opened up a real can of worms that I needed to become far better prepared to deal with.

The following summer, a course entitled "Pastoral Counseling and Spiritual Conflict," taught by Dr. Neil Anderson, was being offered at Trinity. When I tried to enroll, I received word that the course was already full. I then wrote to Dr. Warner, who was also serving as my advisor, and as politely as possible said, "You got me into this, and I need help." The school kindly made room for this desperate missionary from Central America. That course offered many answers, along with the theological and practical balance I was seeking. Wanting to pass that knowledge along to expatriate and national colleagues on the field, I began to develop the seminar upon which a good share of the contents of this book is based.

After returning to the United States in 1991, my interest in spiritual warfare deepened. My wife, Denise, and I found ourselves involved in numerous "deliverance sessions" (something I now prefer to call "freedom appointments" and will explain more in depth in the final section) and teaching. This teaching has taken on various forms and has been offered in the context of high school chapels, Christian school associations, sermon series, retreats, parent groups, youth conventions, and pastors' conferences. I also wrote a course for high school students called *The Battle of the Angels* (CRC Publications).

Having presented some personal history, I should say that my main interest in spiritual warfare lies in the present and the future. I invite you to start, however, where I started—by allowing your worldview to be challenged. In the preface to his book *Spirit Wars,* Peter Jones states:

> On center stage in the war theater that touches everyone is the battle of worldviews. A worldview is what people think when they are least aware—while watching TV or reading the paper. It is at this unconscious level that the struggle is most critical. At the threshold of the third millennium, two radically opposed ways of understanding human nature vie for allegiance . . . like two hockey players poised over the puck, ready to force it in one direction or another."

In the next two chapters we'll look at opposing worldviews and how they affect our day-to-day lives. These worldviews are like filters that we use to screen and process the information we receive about the world. The filtering process is as automatic as the way we brush our teeth, hold our fork, and sign our name. We do it naturally, without being taught. But just as we can change our habits, so we can also change the way we view and react to life as a whole, including the spiritual.

Saint Michael Subdues Satan

—Raphael, 1483-1520

CHAPTER 2

THE WAR BETWEEN WORLDVIEWS

You've received a letter announcing that YOU could be the next lucky winner of TEN MILLION DOLLARS! So, though you normally don't do these things, you decide—just to justify your skepticism—to provide the required information and to place all the stickers in their appropriate places in every stage of the "Publisher's Clearinghouse Sweepstakes." You seriously doubt that you will win, so you haven't made any down payments on a new sports car. But you are convinced that there is a possibility of winning, however remote.

After all, you say to yourself, they publish the names and pictures of previous winners. And well-known celebrities are involved. The Prize Patrol goes out, and winners are interviewed on television. If it were fake, the government would have shut it down long ago, right?

Then one day in January you receive a phone call from someone who identifies himself as Ed McMahon. Ed verifies your name, address, and other information. Then, with great enthusiasm, he informs you that you are the winner of the Clearinghouse's ten million dollar grand prize.

Assuming that you've told no one about your entry (so the voice could not be that of a friend playing a joke), that the caller indeed sounds like Ed McMahon, and that you've been previously notified that you made it to the ranks of the finalists, you could probably be convinced that you had—against overwhelming odds—won ten million dollars. Even though you never expected it to happen, it was not totally removed from your mind's "realm of possibility."

Now let's suppose that Aunt Mildred calls. Aunt Mildred is not exactly what most of your extended family considers to be stable, partially because she goes to a church whose worship is loud and unrestrained and whose beliefs include that of miraculous healing. Aunt Mildred is on the phone excitedly claiming that her lumbago and rheumatoid arthritis were instantly healed at a church prayer service. You simply cannot buy this explanation, so you offer several more rational possibilities, among them a type of psychosomatic healing. After all, you explain, "Prayer can be emotionally calming and psychologically beneficial. But miraculous healing? No, I'm afraid that's a bit much!"

Both scenarios describe events that we probably agree are extremely unlikely, yet many would consider the first more plausible than the second. Even though we may feel that mail-order sweepstakes are not highly reliable nor above suspicion, even though we certainly do not think celebrities and television are good standards for measuring reality, we have, either consciously or unconsciously, accepted them as reliable sources. On the other hand, the only thing that testifies in favor of Aunt Mildred's miraculous healing is the Bible. If accepting the possibility of the healing is harder for us than accepting the possibility of winning ten million dollars, have we judged the Bible to be less reliable (at least in some areas) than sweepstakes, celebrities, and television?

That's harsh, and it may raise your hackles a bit. I hope so. It's a serious statement. When I suggest that many of us—yes, I mean Christians—do not take the Bible seriously, I expect to encounter a certain amount of defensiveness. But I also hope this statement catches your attention. I hope that the notion is disruptive enough to cause you to stop and think about it.

I am not suggesting that we are blatantly disregarding the Word of God. I *am* suggesting, however, that our process of responding to and interpreting the world around us is not always based on what the Bible seems to say at first reading. More and more we find ourselves interpreting, reframing, or "trimming" the biblical text based on other sources of "reality." As I admitted in the last chapter, this was my own subconscious approach to the idea of spiritual warfare.

I am not referring to anything as overt as theologian Rudolf Bultmann's attempts to demythologize Scripture by eradicating anything supernatural or miraculous, such as the virgin birth and Jesus' miracles. I am speaking more of the difference that exists between exegesis and eisegesis. When we exegete (*ex* = out) Scripture, we seek to discover what we can get out of Scripture to apply to a particular context. On the other hand, eisegesis (*eis* = into) occurs when we take preconceived ideas to Scripture and try to force Scripture to fit those notions. We often refer to this as "proof-texting": the art of finding scattered, disassociated, and out-of-context Bible verses to prove a given point. Eisegesis is an inappropriate use of the Word. Most of us, however, practice it on a regular basis by allowing our interpretation of reality to be the filter through which we interpret Scripture. I am not talking about hermeneutical tools such as the historical setting, language, and culture of the biblical era; rather, I am referring to our most obvious modern-day frame of reference, a Western worldview. Allow me a further example:

> Suppose you are a missionary doctor. One day you find yourself speaking with the chief of a remote and rather primitive African village. Suddenly the chief's young daughter starts convulsing. The

chief explains that his daughter is "with spirit" as a result of having been cursed by a neighboring village's witch doctor. He asks you to call upon your God to break the curse and restore her to wholeness. Do you set your medical training aside for the moment and pray for her freedom, or do you ignore this "superstitious nonsense" and treat it as an epileptic seizure, which is what the symptoms clearly seem to indicate?

If our belief system is based only on the spiritual, without giving credence to the physical world in which we live, we tend to blame or attribute all things to spirits, be they bad or good. On the other hand, if our modus operandi is firmly rooted in the physical reality, disallowing anything spiritual, we are not able to operate outside the boundaries of modern science. The Bible clearly recognizes both realities—the physical and the spiritual—and our interaction with them.

> . . . and people brought to [Jesus] all who were ill with various *diseases*, those suffering *severe pain*, the *demon-possessed*, those having *seizures*, and the *paralyzed*, and he healed them (Matt. 4:4).
>
> That evening after sunset the people brought to Jesus all the sick *and* demon-possessed (Mark 1:32, italics mine).

I would guess that most readers of this book would readily, perhaps forcefully, declare their belief in the Bible as the inspired, reliable Word of God. The Heidelberg Catechism, a creedal standard of Reformed churches for centuries, acknowledges the first mark of true faith as being "a knowledge and conviction that everything that God reveals in his Word is true" (Q&A 21). Another doctrinal standard of faith, the Belgic Confession (1561), says that Christians are to believe "without any doubt all things contained in [Scripture], not so much because the Church receives and approves them as such, but more especially because the Holy Spirit witnesses in our hearts that they are from God, and also because they carry the evidence thereof in themselves" (Art. V).

Does our application of Scripture attest to belief beyond doubt? Lesslie Newbigin, missionary statesman and theologian, suggests, "It is less important to ask a Christian what he or she believes about the Bible than it is to inquire what he or she does with it" (Newbigin, *Proper Confidence*, Eerdmans, 1995, p. 105). If we, as the Christian church, desire to effectively answer the call to arms in the realm of spiritual warfare, we must first respond to a wake-up call regarding our worldview.

Defining Worldview

According to Tim Warner, our worldview is "the thought system we develop for explaining the world around us and our experiences in it" (*Spiritual Warfare,*

p. 24). Given this definition, I suppose we could say that each person's worldview is as unique as his or her fingerprints. That's because each individual worldview, in its most personal aspect, is made up of all our past experiences. Those experiences, arrived at by means of formal or informal educational processes, may have been positive or negative, conscious or subconscious, very limited or very broad. Unlike fingerprints, our worldview is subject to constant change because each day brings new experiences into the mix.

There are, however, broader worldview patterns that are shaped by experiences we share with those around us. Missiologists speak of "people groups"—homogeneous units that are identified by what they have in common. Common experiences and backgrounds, shaped by such factors as cultural norms, formal education, ethnicity, and religion, lead us to a common interpretation of and reaction to life. We could refer to this as our "societal worldview."

A brief look at the work of archaeologists and anthropologists can help us understand the concept of worldview. Archaeologists and anthropologists must dig through several layers to arrive at the foundation. The archaeologist searches for the origin of the site under study. Several years ago, workers in Mexico City were digging a tunnel for a new subway line under the central plaza when they discovered what appeared to be Aztec ruins. Archaeologists had long speculated that the hub of the ancient Aztec empire was in the area of Mexico City, but this was the first hint of proof. With careful excavation the remains of an ancient pyramid-style temple emerged. Further digging revealed several more temples, each built over the previous one, and each one marking the establishment of a new king or dynasty. At the lowest level of the dig, archaeologists discovered the original temple and the origin of the Aztec empire in that area.

Anthropologists look for origins or starting points of the societies they study. That starting point is the society's worldview. To arrive there they must "dig" through various layers, such as observable behavior and objects (artifacts), institutions and values (see Figure 1). For instance, a society with a materialistic worldview would base its values on economic impact, develop institutions related to banking and finance, show evidence of leisure-time behavior, and display objects such as houses and personal possessions. A society with a scientific/academic worldview would develop institutions of higher learning and libraries. Its observable behaviors and artifacts would be related to the consuming and distribution of facts.

One would expect that a worldview based on a biblical interpretation of God and the world around us would have an observable relationship to our values, institutions, and behavior. What will anthropologists of the future have to say

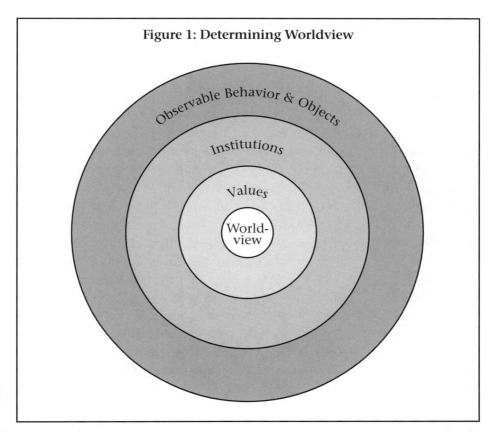

Figure 1: Determining Worldview

Observable Behavior & Objects

Institutions

Values

World-view

about our worldview? Since it might not be fair or accurate to make assumptions about our worldview based upon the observable behavior of society around us, let's be more specific. By studying the behavior, objects, institutions, and values of your present community of believers, what would anthropologists of the future conclude about your worldview? Would the foundation they discover be the Bible? Here again, honest reflection on these questions might bring us up short.

Here's my point: the foundation of our belief system determines how we respond to and act in the world in which we live. If you're not absolutely sure of your belief system, look at your actions. It has been accurately observed that "people may not live what they profess, but they will always live what they believe" (Warner, *Spiritual Warfare*, p. 24).

Opposing Worldviews

Let's look at two seemingly contradictory and opposite belief systems: animism and, for lack of a better term, a Western worldview. I say "seemingly contradictory" because even though they appear to be diametrically opposed to each other, these worldviews have been able to coexist and, in some cases, syncretize quite comfortably. Please keep in mind that these belief systems have many variations and that my treatment here is somewhat simplified.

Animism

If you've ever seen old Tarzan or wild-West movies, you have been exposed to animism. In fact, much of today's entertainment introduces animistic themes (many New Age themes, for example, are sophisticated forms of animism). Whether it's a sacrifice being made to appease the angry spirit of an erupting volcano, a dance to invoke the spirit of rain, the spirit guidance of a dead ancestor, or "the force," the concept presented is that of a spiritual reality that governs, or at least is involved in, much of what happens to and around us. Animism is not a major religion, it does not have a formal belief system, and it is not based upon a holy book. It is based on the assumption that impersonal spiritual power (spirits) exists in all elements: animal, vegetable, and mineral.

According to animism, spirits can be associated with any object of nature, whether animate (such as an animal) or inanimate (a rock, a tree, or an entire mountain). They can also be associated with specific people, dead (ancestor veneration) or alive (shaman, sorcerers, witch doctors, spiritists, or channelers). These spirits can be benevolent or malevolent, and they have varying degrees of strength or weakness. In an animistic system, spirits are involved in all aspects of life. Although the spiritual and natural are not identical, there is no real separation between the two (Figure 2). The spiritual powers constantly intervene in people's lives. Animism may or may not include the concept of a creator god. Within this system, a purely scientific view would be almost incomprehensible because it requires that the physical (the empirically measurable) be separated from the spiritual.

Within this framework, humanity constantly acts or reacts to the interventions of the spirits. So it becomes crucial to determine which spirits are stronger and which are prone to malevolence. One can pretty well ignore spirits that remain weak and/or benevolent; however, much of life is dedicated to appeasing potentially harmful spirits. Often, this process of appeasement must be accomplished by one who can be an intermediary with the spirits (such as a shaman or a witch doctor). Obviously this intermediary can become a very influential and powerful person, and a very elaborate system of appeasement via altars, sacrifices, and ceremonies (religion) can be developed. Everything a person does is determined by how he or she believes the spirits will react.

Picture, by way of example, an animistic people living on a remote island. These people seldom experience natural catastrophes and have few worries other than netting their daily food supply. Such a society is not likely to have

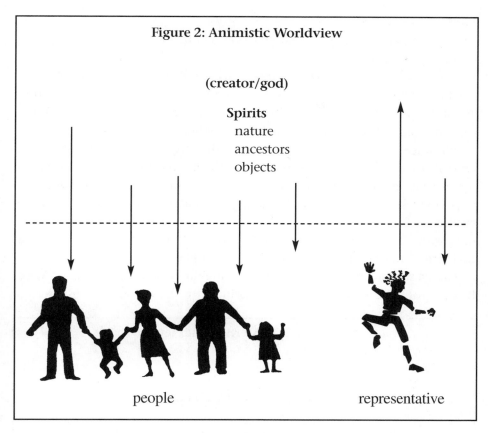

Figure 2: Animistic Worldview

(creator/god)

Spirits
nature
ancestors
objects

people   representative

an elaborately developed religious system. Their intermediary with the spirits, if they have one, will not carry a lot of influence—unless something elemental begins to threaten their peaceful existence.

On the other hand, picture Inuit people living in the northern tundra, trying to survive cruel winters, wild animals, and earthquakes, eking out a food supply during a short and treacherous whaling season. Such people are much more likely to have a fairly complex religious system aimed at appeasing powerful and dangerous spirits. Their intermediary will also be powerful.

Although many people think that animistic beliefs are directly proportional to the level of civilization, that's not the case. It is secularization, not civilization, that has most notably contradicted and vanquished animism, at least on the surface. Secularism involves eliminating the religious element from life, getting rid of God, dumping the idea of spirits. The Western worldview, which we will look at next, is purely secular, just the opposite of animism. Lesslie Newbigin makes the interesting observation that Western Christian missionaries have been one of the most secularizing forces of the twentieth century (Newbigin, *Honest Religion for Secular Man*).

Western Worldview

As you would expect, our Western worldview paints quite a different picture of reality. In it the so-called supernatural (spiritual) realm of religion is totally separated from the supposedly natural (physical) realm of science or man (the solid lines in Figure 3 represent this separation). There's no free-flowing interaction between the two realms; in fact, belief in the "supernatural" is impermanent, something to be eliminated when "enlightenment" no longer requires its existence. For the time being, the two realms are separated by what missiologist Paul Hiebert refers to as the "excluded middle," the realm of spiritual forces that are active in the background, bringing interaction between the realm of God and the realm of humanity (natural science). Obviously, the scientific Western worldview does not accept Dr. Hiebert's definition of this middle ground. It is seen, rather, as a credibility gap that exists between the "natural" and "supernatural" or between science and religion.

The Western worldview was birthed during the period known as the "Age of Reason" or "the Enlightenment," considered to be a period of intellectual

---

Figure 3: Western Worldview

SUPERNATURAL*
Realm of Religion

(EXCLUDED MIDDLE)

NATURAL*
Realm of Science

*Please note that the terms "supernatural" and "natural" are typical of the Western worldview but not of a biblical worldview. They set up a false dualism by suggesting that spiritual matters are somehow not "natural," when in fact spiritual realities are perfectly "natural" because they are part of God's creational work.

---

revival in eighteenth-century Europe. It was a time when rationalism and empirical proof replaced faith as the test of truth. Repeatable confirmation of data measured by the five senses became the only reliable source of knowing and understanding the reality in which we live. The idea is that anything that science cannot explain today will eventually become explainable; it is simply a matter of collecting all the empirical data to properly understand our universe.

Our Western worldview has never proven spiritual reality to be false; it simply makes the a priori assumption that the supernatural does not exist because it cannot be tested by natural laws. Let me say that again, in another way. A Western worldview assumes the existence of only the natural and natural laws; since the supernatural cannot be measured by natural laws (that, by the way, is why they call it "supernatural"), it must not exist. We do well to wonder what is so "enlightening" about such circular logic.

Allow me to demonstrate how this works. In the Western worldview, belief in the supernatural is sometimes referred to as the "God of the gaps," the gaps representing areas that science has not yet explained. In the absence of rational, scientific explanation, these instances (such as Jesus' resurrection) were thrown into the realm of the supernatural. For instance, before we understood what caused earthquakes, we assumed they were the result of God's (or a sprit's) anger and punishment. When we developed a greater understanding of earthquakes and their causes, however, the supernatural (God, the spirits) was no longer needed to explain them. As the gaps in understanding became smaller and fewer, the need for God began to diminish.

That's why, in the early 1960s, liberalism claimed that God was dead—dead because God was no longer needed. In the euphoria of successful moon launches and rapid technological advancement, some declared that we were on the very brink of knowing everything there was to know. Less than one generation after that smug declaration, however, scientists now estimate that although our knowledge has more than doubled, we still have a long way to go. The more we know and understand, the more we realize we don't know. God was revived, if for nothing more than the psychological benefits that belief could bring.

You will notice that Figure 3 includes no connectors between the realm of God and the realm of science. Our Western worldview says it's okay to believe in God if you need that psychological crutch, but there's simply no rational way to arrive at that belief. To arrive at the realm of God you have to take what philosopher Immanuel Kant has referred to as "a blind leap of faith."

In part, the age of enlightenment was a reaction against the Middle Ages and its exaggerated theologies and theories about the spiritual world (remember the infamous debate about how many angels could dance on head of a pin?). Paul

Hiebert describes the resulting worldview as the mystification of religion and the secularization of science. So this worldview leaves us with two functional realities: the supernatural, to which belong God and other spiritual beings; and the natural, to which belongs the created world, functioning within the parameters of natural laws. All our questions must have "either/or" answers; everything must be either natural or supernatural, scientific or religious, psychological or religious. A.W. Tozer describes this as a totally unnecessary but common habit of dividing our lives into two areas—the sacred and the secular. He says this division is one of the greatest hindrances to a Christian's internal peace (Tozer, *The Pursuit of God*, Christian Publications, 1948, p. 105).

The empty, excluded middle has eliminated our link to God. Since the spiritual realm and the physical realm have no functional connection, our Western worldview requires us to take that leap of faith when dealing with occurrences (such as the rare miracle) that the natural can't yet explain. A newsmagazine survey of a few years ago showed that 87 percent of those polled believe in a created world, but they think that world is totally governed by natural laws without supernatural intervention. This leads Tim Warner to describe Western-worldview Christians as functional deists, believing that God created the world and its natural laws and then let it run on its own without intervention.

You will note that I have consistently described the Western worldview as "our" worldview, identifying ourselves with this frame of reference, this system of belief regarding the natural and supernatural. For some of us that may be highly offensive. We are men and women of faith. We believe in an omniscient (all-knowing), omnipresent (everywhere present), omnipotent (all-powerful) God. Our God is alive, well, and active in the world today. We accept God, and we accept God's Word. If that's so, why do we automatically struggle with some of the issues presented at the beginning of this chapter? Why did I, as a Bible-believing Christian, struggle with the concept of the demonic and the literalness of spiritual warfare?

It's because most of us have been, at least to some degree, shaped by a Western worldview. This worldview is the pair of glasses we wear and through which we see reality, even though the glasses are lightly tinted by our religious convictions. Even though we read our Bible and claim it as truth, even though we attend a fellowship of faith regularly, even though some of us were educated in Christian institutions that taught us to integrate Christianity into daily life, most of us were raised in a society based on a Western worldview.

This worldview has influenced us more than we sometimes admit. For instance, we claim to believe in a miracle-working God, yet when faced with a miracle we automatically (and sometimes frantically) look for the plausible, rational explanation. We may feel uncomfortable stepping into the world of the supernatural and the unexplainable. Knowledge gives power, and power gives control. We lose control and are definitely out of our comfort zone when things can't be accounted for within a worldview with which we've become (even if subconsciously) comfortable.

Please do not misunderstand me on this point. I believe that our ability to reason is part of our identity as imagebearers of God. Our God is a rational, reasoning God who has created in us the capacity for thought and reason. God expects us to use that capacity to its fullest extent. But God doesn't expect it to become our master, especially if it is bounded by the parameters of naturalistic understanding. Limiting ourselves to the confines of naturalistic understanding can and has led to the situation that God describes through the prophet, Jeremiah:

> I remember the devotion of your youth,
> how as a bride you loved me. . . .
> Now they say to wood, "You are my father,"
> and to stone, "You gave me birth."
> They have turned their backs to me and not their faces.
>
> —Jeremiah 2:3, 27

Here's the simple truth: if we want to fully benefit from our ability to reason, we've got to place that ability within the proper system. That system is a biblical worldview, the topic of the next chapter.

The Birth of Shame, detail

—Julius Schnorr Von Carolsfeld, 1749-1872

CHAPTER 3

DRAMA IN REAL LIFE

Several years ago, while living in Costa Rica, our family was involved in a stage production of *The Sound of Music*. We all had parts, except our youngest daughter, but she was as immersed as any of us in the rehearsals, learning lines, and memorizing music. I remember her, then only nine years old, running around the house singing the alto part of the Latin chants that corresponded to my wife's role as a nun. I am also convinced that she knew every line in the entire play.

If you've been involved in a theatrical production, you soon realize that there's much more going on than what the audience can see. Often more activity takes place behind the scenes than on stage. Crew members run the sound and lighting, change the props, get costuming ready, fix makeup and, when necessary, even cue the actors on their lines. The crew is totally dedicated to assisting those on stage in whatever way necessary so that the production comes off as written.

In somewhat the same way, a tremendous amount of behind-the-scenes spiritual activity is part of the reality in which we live. Reality is not limited to what our five senses experience. A purely Western worldview does not allow us to deal effectively with reality. Only a biblical worldview can do that.

A Biblical Worldview

The Bible can be thought of as a drama—the unfolding history of God's relationship with a chosen people. Early on we see that God developed a personal relationship with our first parents. Even when humanity broke that relationship, God deliberately planned to restore it. But God's plan went far beyond one couple; in fact, it was global in scope. As the drama of the Bible unfolds, we see God's plan being worked out through an individual (Abraham), then through a nation (Israel). Eventually this plan extends to every tribe and language on earth (Rev. 5:9). The primary stage for the drama is the earth, introduced in the opening verses of Genesis.

The Bible does not give an abundance of information about the spiritual activity going on behind the scenes (at least when you consider percentage of content). The main character—God— is not even formally introduced; in fact, the biblical drama begins by simply assuming that the spiritual exists. Genesis does not say, "In the beginning, God . . ." and then go on to explain who God is, where God came from, and so forth. Rather, it simply states what God did—

God created the earth, which was part of a broader universe, and in that environment God planned to create and relate with humankind. As someone observed, Genesis (the Bible) is not a book by man about God; it is a book by God about man.

While the Bible's main intent is not to focus on the spiritual "crew" and the backstage area, neither is it completely silent about the spiritual. A good number of passages refer to the heavens, paint pictures of God seated in majesty, and tell of the deeds of angelic beings that guard gates, lay waste to enemy armies, sing songs, and are the instruments of final judgement.

John Calvin properly warns us against creating elaborate theories about angels from scant biblical information, but the Bible does tell us that the realm of angels exists and that there's significant interaction between the realm of God and the realm of man (Figure 4).

The dotted lines on the diagram represent the interaction between the realms. While the Godhead is the sole, permanent occupant of the realm of God, angels do appear in God's presence as they interact with the realm of humanity, according to God's command and our need. And the Spirit directly links the two realms by being present in the hearts and lives of believers and by working in creation. Of course the diagram is far too restrictive. Obviously, God is not a prisoner of the heavenly realm, sending angels back and forth to us like heavenly carrier pigeons doing his bidding, nor is the structure of the heavenly realm(s) as simplistic as pictured.

The stars and the large and small triangles on the diagram suggest a hierarchy in the angelic ranks (the Bible gives very little information on this structure). Notice that good and evil angels are represented and that angels are active in the realm of humanity. While the Bible gives us plenty of warning about Satan and his followers (fallen angels/demons), it doesn't give us much background information. Apparently that information isn't necessary for us to know in the unfolding drama of God's plan.

Still, a number of passages do describe continuing behind-the-scenes spiritual battles:

- 2 Peter 2:4; Jude 6; John 8:44; and 1 John 3:8 refer to angels sinning and being punished and link Satan to the "beginning."

- Revelation 14:8 and 17:5 make Babylon almost synonymous with evil. Some scholars think that the prophesies concerning the king of Babylon in Isaiah 14 and the king of Tyre in Ezekiel 28 serve a dual purpose in that they also describe the fall of Satan (this conviction dates at least as far back at the third century to the writings of Origen; it is the Latin *Vulgate* that first translates the Hebrew term for "morning star" as Lucifer*). The Ezekiel passage

Figure 4: Biblical Worldview

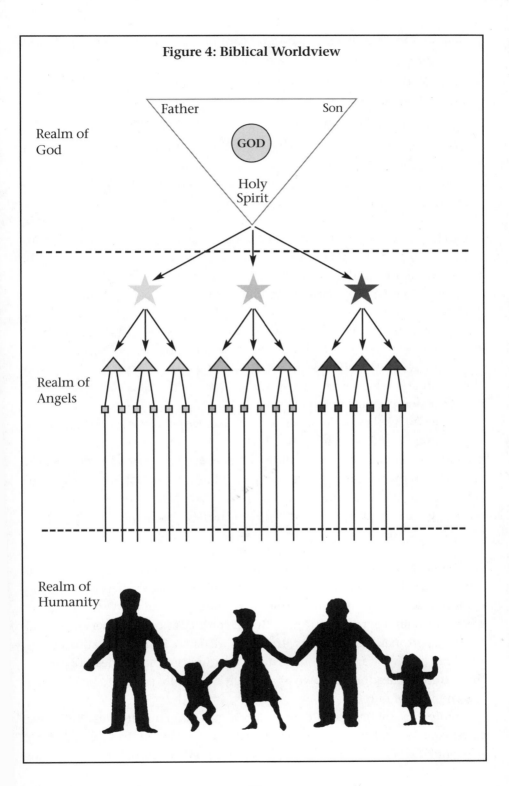

describes Satan as having had significant power (that of an archangel) and prestige in the presence of God.

- Jesus refers to the fall of Satan (Luke 10:18), as does the apocalyptic description of Revelation 12:4.

Since the fall of Satan, much of the battle seems to have shifted to earth, with God's creation, especially humankind, becoming Satan's main target in an attempt to thwart God's plan and steal God's glory.

While we don't know exact numbers, we do know that angelic beings are numerous. At Christ's birth "a great company of the heavenly host appeared" (Luke 2:13). Angelic creatures parade through the book of Revelation in nearly every chapter. Unfortunately, demonic forces (fallen angels) are also numerous. Many assume from the demons' own self-identification as "Legion" that the Gadarene demoniac alone hosted at least a thousand (Mark 5:9).

Figure 5 gives a little more detail about the activity of the realm of angels and the interaction between realms. It would seem that the principal function of angels is to do God's bidding in service to us. Angels are God's heavenly backstage crew that assists in making sure the drama goes according to script (a script that seems to undergo continuous editing by our prayers). A key part of this spiritual interaction is the two-way activity of the Holy Spirit that brings God to us and presents us to God.

It's clear that believers do not escape involvement in the spiritual battle that's raging around us. Ephesians 6:10-12 lets us know in no uncertain terms that our battles will be fought on a spiritual plane, against spiritual forces. We can expect Satan to attack us, either directly or indirectly. Our task is to resist Satan's attacks using "the full armor of God." With God's protection and with God's authority, we can "take [our] stand against the devil's schemes."

Finding Balance

A biblical worldview can give us that crucial balance between pure animism and a naturalistic Western worldview—not only because it offers a satisfactory compromise but because it offers truth in dealing with reality. We want to avoid a fatalistic animism that portrays all things spiritual as being impersonal, disallowing a personal, creator-God with whom we have a personal relationship. At the same time we want to avoid a fatalistic naturalism that denies God or anything spiritual, leading us down a path that eventually proves to be meaningless and void of purpose.

Holding a biblical worldview allows us—as church and individual Christians—to realize all the wonders of the natural world God created and to make full use of our God-given reason to interpret all that nature and creation

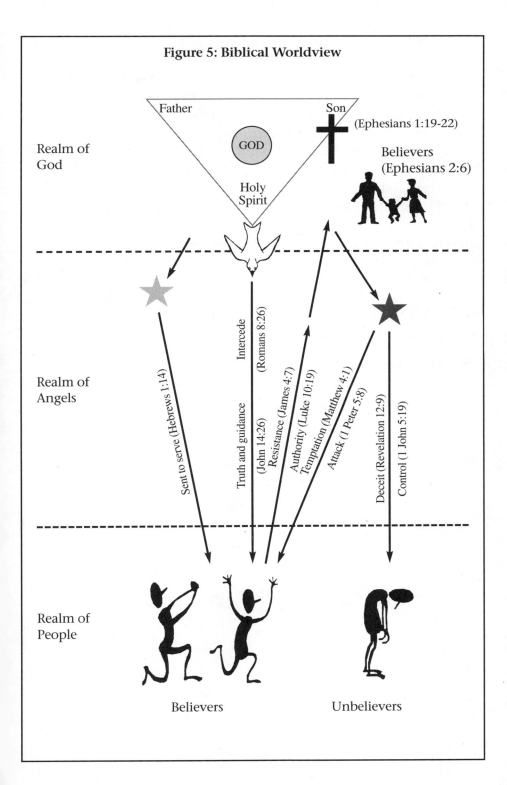

Figure 5: Biblical Worldview

Realm of God

Father

Son

(Ephesians 1:19-22)

GOD

Believers
(Ephesians 2:6)

Holy
Spirit

Realm of Angels

Sent to serve (Hebrews 1:14)

Intercede (Romans 8:26)

Truth and guidance (John 14:26)

Resistance (James 4:7)

Authority (Luke 10:19)

Temptation (Matthew 4:1)

Attack (1 Peter 5:8)

Deceit (Revelation 12:9)

Control (1 John 5:19)

Realm of People

Believers

Unbelievers

have to teach us. In order to hold such a view, we need to recognize that we are created beings with the potential for personally relating with our creator. We need to recognize that our physical reality is set in a broader spiritual reality with which we interact on a constant basis. Teilhard de Chardin once stated that "we are not human beings having a spiritual experience; rather, we are spiritual beings having a human experience."

Figure 6 shows how some churches lean one way or the other. Some tend to be so spiritually minded that the physical is all but ignored; it may even be considered sinful, something to be shunned. For these believers everything has a spiritual cause; their Christianity focuses inward on the development of personal spirituality and spiritual experiences. There is little salt and light interaction within the everyday areas of their lives. Leaning the other way produces liberalism that denies God's active hand in the world today and reduces Christianity and faith to psychological warm fuzzies and positive strokes that "belief" (in almost anything) can give. Our goal is to find the balance of a solid biblical worldview that allows us to live and function with both the spiritual and physical aspects of reality.

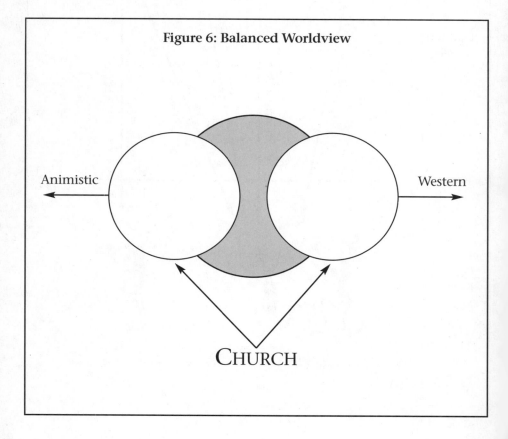

Figure 6: Balanced Worldview

Animistic ← → Western

CHURCH

It is interesting to note that our North American society is experiencing a significant shift in worldview. As the West influences more and more non-Western societies, so too there has been a reverse influence. Many people from countries and cultures based on some form of animism have embraced the wonders of science and technology without denying their formation in the spiritual. Neil Anderson suggests that the whole of the Western world is experiencing a massive worldview shift, as evidenced by the rise in interest in New Age philosophies and practice, parapsychology, the popularity of dabbling in all things supernatural, and overt Satanism (*The Bondage Breaker*, p. 27).

How do we adopt a biblical worldview? I'm not just talking about professing our belief in the Bible as the Word of God, which contains principles we ought to apply in the shaping of our values and our daily lives. I am talking about accepting and applying *all* the principles of the Bible to our system of values and our response to life. While a biblical worldview recognizes spiritual reality, it does not deny science. It does, however, deny that science provides the litmus test of the veracity of the Bible. A biblical worldview filters our science, our reasoning, our systems of logic, all that we accept as true and possible—through the grid of truth found in the Word. Of course, this all depends on an accurate, Spirit-led interpretation of Scripture. We don't deny that the earth is round because Scripture speaks of "the four corners of the earth." We also shouldn't deny the presence and activity of angels and demons because we have no scientific proof of them or because a Western worldview casts them off as nonsense.

Lesslie Newbigin suggests, and I believe rightly so, that Christianity's problem is not with science but with a worldview that began with the Enlightenment and caused what he refers to as a conversion of a culture by "[shifting] the location of reliable truth from the story told in the Bible to the eternal truths of reason, of which the mathematical physics of Newton offered the supreme model" (*Proper Confidence*). We need to shift our location of truth back to the Bible. If we don't, we will be without a belief system that provides the foundation necessary to effectively do battle in the spiritual arena.

Shifting to a biblical worldview brings real benefits. First, it allows active participation in spiritual warfare; second, it changes our expectations of God (this can have a dramatic effect on our prayer life); and, third, it allows for a closer, richer walk with God. This is relational and defines us as Christians.

So how do we go about changing our worldview? To answer that question, we need to look more closely at how worldviews are formed.

Worldview Filters

The illustration in Figure 7 shows how our worldview (and our concept of God) is formed. The various arrows represent input or information received from any source. The ovals represent basic filtering systems in our lives (more filters exist than are shown on the diagram). The first and foremost filter is our **primary belief system.** Most of us in the Western world base our primary belief system on scientific naturalism. As Christians, however, our primary belief system must also include the Word of God. So how does this work? Since "angel stories" are popular these days, let's use them as an example. With the Bible as part of your primary belief system, you would be inclined to allow a story you've heard regarding an angelic appearance to pass through your first filter. While that would not necessarily be true for everybody, a part of you acknowledges the possibility that the story is true.

Our next major filter is that of **experience**—that to which we personally can attest or that we can infer from reliable sources. Let's use the angel example once more. Suppose you had an experience that there is absolutely no other explanation for than the intervention of an angel. The validity of angelic existence breezes right through your "experience" filter. You believe it because it happened to you! But suppose you never had an encounter with an angel, at least that you're aware of. But your pastor, for whom you have high regard, has

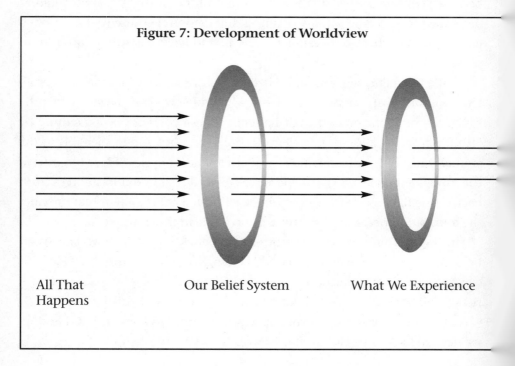

Figure 7: Development of Worldview

All That Happens   Our Belief System   What We Experience had such an experience. Because your pastor is a reliable source, you would probably be inclined to accept his story as true, at least conditionally.

The last basic filter is that of **analysis.** In Western society we have been trained, both through formal and informal education, to analyze facts within scientific and naturalistic parameters. It is built into us. It is what causes us to pause in our thinking. It causes the uncomfortable tension when we face the miraculous or supernatural. Angels, spirits, and other things unexplainable often cannot pass through our analytical filter.

As you see in Figure 7, not much of the original information makes it through the filtering process unscathed. The things that do make it through make up our worldview or our view of reality. Unfortunately, that also defines God for us. Too often our worldview produces a small concept of God. Though God may be nicely packaged, wrapped, and tied in formal religion, God remains almost impotent. Our goal should be to let God out of this box. Not just to crack it open at Sunday worship but to get rid of the box. It's hard to imagine what that could do to the vibrancy of our Christian experience, to the expectancy of our prayer life, to our active involvement in spiritual warfare.

A. W. Toner speaks of a type of Christianity that is in vogue. It is a Christianity that recognizes Christ's presence as theory but not as present reality. He describes a veil in our hearts that effectively shuts out the light and hides

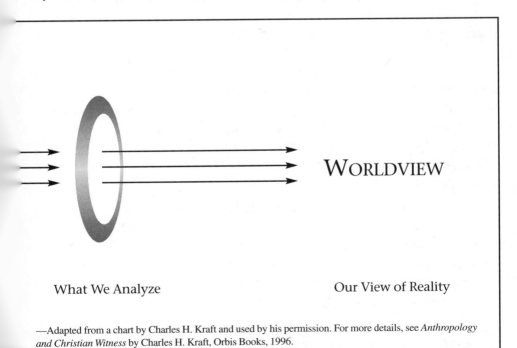

WORLDVIEW

What We Analyze   Our View of Reality

—Adapted from a chart by Charles H. Kraft and used by his permission. For more details, see *Anthropology and Christian Witness* by Charles H. Kraft, Orbis Books, 1996.

the face of God from us (Toner, *The Pursuit of God*). A dramatic change in world-view (letting God out of the box) does wonders in removing that veil.

Please do not misunderstand my suggestion. I am not proposing that we toss out scientific investigation. Neither am I suggesting that we avoid careful critique or thoughtful analysis, as if they somehow are in direct antithesis to knowing biblical truth. God has revealed himself to us in the Word *and* in creation. God created us in his image. That image includes the ability to think and analyze. Creation, which embodies the laws of nature and science, and our minds, which allow us to understand that creation (and understand more of God), are gifts. We simply may *not* throw them aside. While the apostle Paul calls us not to conform to the pattern of this world (its worldview), he does tells us to be transformed by the renewing of our minds (not the *removing* of our minds!).

Figure 8 shows us the desired outcome. Many Christians include a biblical point of reference as part of their belief system, but, by default, have submitted it to the litmus test of a Western worldview. What I propose is simple. We need to reverse the order. We need to give superiority to the truth of the Bible. Everything else must be submitted to its authority. Granted, the Bible is not and was never intended to be a science textbook. But when the Bible and science both speak to the same issue, the Bible speaks the final word. Obviously, proper hermeneutics must be applied to the reading and interpretation of the Bible. But let's be careful not to seek loopholes. Hermeneutics is simply another science that must be submitted to the guidance of the Holy Spirit. So, once again, we're back to our worldview.

How do we go about reversing something that has become almost second nature to us? How do we turn a rushing river so that the current flows in the opposite direction? That is exactly what practicing a biblical worldview will sometimes feel like in our Western society. To a certain degree it's simply a matter of consciously choosing to acknowledge God's Word as truth and to understand that truth. Allow me to suggest some steps toward putting a biblical worldview into practice:

- We can choose to be open to biblical truths that we cannot understand or have not personally experienced. Maybe we've never encountered overt demonic attack, but we can choose to be open to its existence, requesting discernment when we hear others speak of it, even though it "blows our mind" and stretches our comfort zone. If the Bible speaks to something, we can safely seek to understand that thing with an open mind.

- We can choose to risk stepping into unknown territory and perhaps experiencing ridicule. In considering risks, however, we must be careful that we do

Figure 8: Reversing Our Worldview

$$\frac{\text{WESTERN WORLDVIEW}}{\text{BIBLICAL WORLDVIEW}}$$

$$\frac{\text{BIBLICAL WORLDVIEW}}{\text{WESTERN WORLDVIEW}}$$

. . . be transformed by the renewing of your mind.

not enter into areas forbidden by God's Word. An appropriate risk could be something such as asking God for miraculous healing (you don't even have to wait until it's the last resort), or using the name of Jesus to come against what may be a spiritual attack in your life or the life of someone else.

- We can choose to be countercultural in our actions, thought processes, and values. Jesus told us to expect to feel "out of it" when we practice a biblical worldview. We can choose not to allow society's frame of reference for truth to be the gauge by which we measure reality. G. K. Chesterton once commented that "a dead thing can go with the stream, but only a living thing can go against it." Being countercultural by choosing to accept God's Word at face value can be life-giving.

- We can step out in faith. I don't mean the "blind leap" suggested by a Western worldview. Our faith is based upon what we know of God, on God's faithfulness that we have seen demonstrated in our own life, and on the unexplainable trust that the Holy Spirit instills into our hearts and minds. Faith is a funny thing; we don't expend it. The more we use it, the more it grows. Faith in God will allow us to place faith in God's Word. Faith in God's Word will allow us to develop a truly biblical worldview.

Satan and Demons

We have now come full cycle. The initial question of this section was, "Do Satan and demons exist, and are they active in the world today?"

Jesus told his disciples that Satan had requested permission to sift them like wheat (Luke 22:31). Even though Jesus was addressing Simon Peter, the "you" in this verse is plural in the original text. Jesus was speaking to all the disciples. This tells me that Jesus is also speaking to us. If we are going to readily accept the promises and blessings that the biblical writers penned or that Jesus spoke to his disciples, we also have to accept the responsibilities, challenges, and warnings. Earlier, Jesus told his disciples (us) that [we] have been given authority to overcome all the power of the enemy (Satan) (Luke 10:19).

Peter remembers what Jesus once told him and passes the warning along, describing Satan as our enemy—a prowling lion lurking about in search of someone to devour (1 Pet. 5:8). John reminds us of spirits that do not acknowledge Jesus as Lord and that even though we have victory, Satan is still in the world (1 John 4:4). Finally, Paul sets the Ephesian believers straight concerning their (our) real battle:

> Finally, be strong in the Lord and in his mighty power. Put on the full armor of God so that you can take your stand against the devil's schemes. For our struggle is not against flesh and blood, but against the rulers, against the authorities, against the powers of this dark world and against the spiritual forces of evil in the heavenly realms. Therefore put on the full armor of God, so that when the day of evil comes, you may be able to stand your ground, and after you have done everything, to stand. (Eph. 6:10-13)

If we agree that the Bible speaks to us today, we cannot help but conclude that Satan and demonic forces are active realities to be dealt with in today's world. If this is so obvious, why a whole section on worldview? Simply because—though we know what the Bible says—we've been programmed by a worldview that, at worst, denies anything spiritual or beyond physical reality, and at best depersonalizes Satan and demons or explains them away as filling the "gaps" in the biblical authors' (and Jesus') scientific understanding. We can profess belief in the Bible and even in the present reality of Satan and his demonic host; however, when we face spiritual warfare, we will not be prepared to do battle unless our worldview is guided and governed by scriptural truth. Calvin's warning still stands:

> The tendency of all that Scripture teaches concerning devils [demons] is to put us on our guard against their wiles and machinations, that we may provide ourselves with weapons strong enough to drive away the most formidable foes. For when Satan is called the god and ruler of this world, the strong man armed, the prince of the power of the air, the roaring lion, the object of all these descriptions is to make us more cautious and vigilant and more prepared for the contest. . . . Being forewarned of the constant presence of an enemy

the most daring, the most powerful, the most crafty, the most inde-fatigable, the most completely equipped with all the engines, and the most expert in the science of war, let us not allow ourselves to be overtaken by sloth or cowardice, but, on the contrary, with minds aroused and ever on the alert, let us stand ready to resist; and, know-ing that this warfare is terminated only by death, let us study to per-severe.

That we may feel the more strongly urged to do so, the Scripture declares that the enemies who war against us are not one or two, or a few in number, but a great host. (Calvin's *Institutes*, I, XIV, 13-14)

So, yes, we face the reality of Satan and demons today. But does that fact make any difference to Christian believers? Can Satan and/or demons attack Christians? That is an important question and is the theme of our next section.

---

* Opinion differs widely on the interpretation of the Isaiah 14 and Ezekiel 28 passages. Calvin states that to suppose that Isaiah 14:12ff refers to Satan "arises from ignorance; for the context clearly shows that these statements must be understood in reference to the king of the Babylonians" (Calvin, *Calvin's Commentaries*, Volume VII, Isaiah 1-32, p. 442). H. A. Ironside, on the other hand, states, "These words cannot apply to any mere mortal man. Lucifer (the light-bearer) is a created angel of the very highest order, identical with the covering cherub of Ezekiel 28. He was, apparently, the greatest of all the angel host and was perfect before God until he fell through pride. It was his ambition to take the throne of Deity for himself and become the supreme ruler of the universe" (Ironside, *The Prophet Isaiah*, pp. 88-89). Wayne Gruden suggests, and I agree, that there may be a double meaning in these passages, using an event in the past (Satan's fall) as prophetic style. (Gruden, *Systematic Theology*, p. 413). A very similar style of double intent was used by the same prophet earlier in reference to the sign given to king Ahaz (7:14ff).

REFLECTION ON CHAPTERS 1-3

This section is intended for individual reflection and/or group discussion.

Bible Study

Read Genesis 3:1-4, 12; Luke 22:31, 32; Job 1:6-12; 2:1-7

1. What similarities do you see in Satan's activity or desire in these passages?

2. What differences do you see in the way Satan attacked Eve and the way Satan attacked Job?

Read John 17:15; Ephesians 6:10-13

3. After reading these passages, take about one minute to jot down a list of words or phrases that the passages bring to mind.

4. In John 17:15, who does "them" refer to? Why do they need protection?

5. Is the advice in Ephesians 6 intended for the church in Ephesus or for us today?

General Discussion

1. Have you had a personal experience involving angels (good or evil) that you've not felt comfortable sharing with anyone? If so, write about that experience in as much detail as you can remember, so that you can better think it through. When you feel able to share that experience with someone else, do so.

2. Give an example of how a Western worldview influences your life. In what way has that influence had a positive or negative effect on your Christian walk?

3. Give an example of how a biblical worldview influences your life.

4. In what ways have you seen the church lose balance by overreacting to or being too accepting of a Western worldview?

5. Satan is a fearsome adversary who attacks us ruthlessly. In the face of satanic power and evil, where do you find comfort and strength? Is there a Bible passage or story that comes to mind? Or something from another source?

A Reading

As followers of Jesus Christ,
living in this world—
which some seek to control, but which others view with despair—
we declare with joy and trust:
Our world belongs to God!

Our world belongs to God—
not to us or earthly powers,
not to demons, fate, or chance.
The earth is the Lord's!

. . . God is present in our world
by his Word and Spirit.
The faithfulness
of our great Provider
gives sense to our days
and hope to our years.
The future is secure,
for our world belongs to God.

—*Our World Belongs to God: A Contemporary Testimony*, stanzas 1, 7, 13

QUESTION 2

Can Satan or demons attack Christians?

Temptation of Christ in the Wilderness

—Juan de Flandes, fl. 1496-c.1519

CHAPTER 4

SATAN'S INTEREST IN THE BATTLE

In the first three chapters, we asked if Satan and demons exist and are active in today's world. If we admit, albeit begrudgingly and with dismay, that Satan and his demonic forces are indeed alive and well, several other questions present themselves:

- Where is Satan?

- What can Satan do?

- How does Satan do these things?

- Who can Satan attack?

- Am I in danger?

- How immediate is that danger?

- How serious is that danger?

We do well to ask these questions. We would ask the same questions about *any* potential danger or enemy that confronts us.

If we continue our analogy of warfare, we should be asking the kinds of questions a general might ask in the face of an encroaching enemy force. The general would want to know the lay of the land—the location, size, and shape of the battlefield. While much of the action in spiritual warfare is behind-the-scenes, a considerable amount of the action takes place right here, on earth. The battle is here and now. Though that may sound like a home court advantage, remember that our enemy is prince of this world. Satan understands its darkness very well and knows how to wield the evil that has become a natural part of our world. We can expect Satan to use that environment to gain offensive and defensive advantage and to camouflage his movements and activity. We'll discuss this further in chapter 7 when we look at the relationship between our three primary enemies: the flesh, the world, and Satan.

Another immediate question a general might ask is, "How strong is this enemy force?" We know from Scripture that Satan was created as a higher-authority angelic being. Nowhere do we read that Satan's power was diminished by his fall from grace. Even though we may wonder why God did not strip Satan of his power and authority, our wondering doesn't change the fact that Satan remains an extremely powerful enemy. No amount of wishing it weren't so or living in denial is going to reduce Satan's might. Knowing the battlefield and the strength of the enemy is important, but we also need to know the enemy's intent and limitations. If we discovered that this army massed at our frontier did not intend to wage war against us, we would probably choose not to rush out on the offensive. We would probably adopt a "cold war" mentality. Or if this army, regardless of how strong, was not able to get at us due to some natural obstacle or to lack of resources to wage a long-term conflict, our concern would be significantly reduced.

For these reasons, we must move beyond simply acknowledging Satan's existence to ask if Satan and his demons are capable of attacking Christians. If the presence of the Holy Spirit and the blood of Christ protect us in such a way that Satan and demons literally can do us no harm, we need not be overly concerned. However, a total lack of concern would be quite selfish. Even if Satan were limited to attacking unbelievers and corrupting only secular society, the church could not turn away unconcerned. (Still, we must admit that if the attack isn't directed against us personally, we can breathe a major sigh of relief.)

In this chapter we'll deal with the question of Satan's intent or his interest in the battle. Why would Satan even want to attack Christians? Before doing that, we need to look at what Scripture has to say about what it means to be a Christian.

Who We Are as Christians

A Christian is someone who—by faith and by the grace of God—is pardoned, reconciled, and adopted by God. The apostle Paul writes to the believers at Colosse:

> When you were dead in your sins and in the uncircumcision of your sinful nature, God made you alive with Christ. He forgave us all our sins, having canceled the written code, with its regulations, that was against us and that stood opposed to us; he took it away, nailing it to the cross. And having disarmed the powers and authorities, he made a public spectacle of them, triumphing over them by the cross. (Col. 2:13-15)

As a Christian, you have been forgiven all your sins. Your debt of sin has been canceled by Christ's blood, and the law of God no longer stands to condemn you. One of the most poignant pictures in Scripture is that of Satan standing at the right hand of Joshua, the high priest, in order to accuse him before the angel of the Lord. Satan is attempting to use the standards of righteousness as laid out in the law to denounce Joshua. It is Satan, however, not Joshua, who is rebuked by the angel of the Lord (many scholars identify the angel of the Lord as Christ), and Joshua is reminded that his sin has been taken away (Zech. 3:1-4). Jesus clearly says that his blood has been poured out for your forgiveness (Matt. 26:28). Because you have recognized Jesus Christ as your only and fully sufficient Savior, you are fully forgiven and declared righteous. This single, glorious truth is essential to your identity as a Christian.

As a Christian, you are not only forgiven, you are also reconciled. Paul declares that the cause of our rejoicing is our reconciliation with God through Jesus Christ (Rom. 5:11). Reconciliation means that a right relationship has been restored. Christianity, in its essence, is a relationship, not a religion, and the Bible is a pictorial history of God in relationship with God's people. The book of Hosea paints an especially moving picture of reconciliation, of God working to mend a broken relationship. God declares that the children previously known as "not loved" and "not my people" will be loved and called "my people" (1:6-9; 2:1) and that the wayward bride will be tenderly received (3:1). This is the picture that Peter has in mind when he describes the church (Christians) as once not being a people nor receiving mercy but now, in Christ, being declared to be God's own (1 Pet. 2:10).

Another building block of your identity as a Christian is that you are a child of God (John 1:12). If you are a child, according to Paul, then you are also an heir— an heir of God and a co-heir with Christ (Rom. 8:17).

Finally, you are adopted. Adoption is a legal matter that goes well beyond guardianship or foster care. It implies legal rights. It implies inheritance and participation. It implies identity. Paul tells the Galatian believers that Christ came to remove us from the foster care of the law and to give us our rights as God's children. Because of Christ, you may call God "Daddy." As a co-heir with Christ you share in his victory (Rom. 8:37), and you mysteriously have been seated with him (present reality) in a position of authority in the heavenly realms (Eph. 2:6). This is your identity in Christ. This is your belt of truth. This is your shield of faith. This is your helmet of salvation.

Neil Anderson has compiled a wonderful list of scriptural truths entitled "Who Am I in Christ?" (See Appendix A). I recommend that you refer to it often as a "reality check," so that when the accuser stands by your side you can rebuke him with the Word of truth.

Why Satan Attacks

The vivid imagery of the dragon in Revelation 12 and the roaring lion in 1 Peter 5:8 depicts a powerful foe who sets out to utterly destroy. What Satan hopes to do is obvious—unable to destroy (devour) the child, he seeks to destroy the child's message and influence. It is Satan's goal to eliminate the gospel message and to destroy its primary conveyors—the body of Christ. While we need to understand how Satan attempts to destroy, we should first gain some insight into his motivation.

Why would Satan *want* to attack us? Military commanders must constantly measure potential gains against potential losses. If we belong to God and our identity and position are sealed by Christ's blood and guaranteed by the Holy Spirit, why would Satan bother? Would it not be far more advantageous to focus on those who are weak, powerless, and vulnerable, rather than to mess with those who share in the very authority of Jesus Christ and are gifted with the presence and power of the Spirit of God?

In answering the "why" question, we need to recognize that Satan, while a spiritual being, is also endowed with personality. Like us, Satan can be angry— angry enough to seek vengeance. Like us, Satan can be prideful—proud enough to relentlessly pursue his own glory. As with us, the combination of anger and pride can lead to irrational responses. Let's look first at Satan's anger and desire for vengeance.

Allow me a homely illustration that I believe I first heard on a tape of a seminar on spiritual warfare at a John Maxwell conference. Suppose that your teenage daughter is madly in love. The signs are all there—she's living in "la-la land," just barely aware of the reality taking place around her, and her thoughts are focused only on "Mr. Right" day and night. One evening she comes home from a date with Mr. Right, slams the door shut, and stomps off to her room. In addition to the slamming and stomping, you are quite sure you also heard sobbing. You guessed it—Mr. Right has suddenly become Mr. Wrong, and your daughter is facedown on her bed sobbing uncontrollably. In the midst of her torrent of tears she turns her head and happens to notice on the dresser a picture of Mr. Right in a frame adorned with golden hearts. A sudden stillness sweeps over her. She quietly rises, walks over to the dresser, gently picks up the picture, and gazes intently at the image. Suddenly she throws the frame to the floor, stomps on it, breaks the glass, removes the picture, and tears it into shreds. She then breathes a deep sigh of relief and begins to do her homework.

What happened? Consider this: she wanted to hurt her boyfriend, but he wasn't there. So she did the next best thing—she attacked his image. There is relief in that gesture. If he knew of the attack he would probably be hurt.

Now let's back up. Satan was a guardian cherub, referred to as the morning star (Lucifer). He was a model of perfection, full of wisdom and beauty, in the presence of God on the mount of God. But because of his aspirations to rise above God and to rob God of his glory, Satan was cast down to the earth. He and his followers did not attain their quest for further glory; in fact, they lost what splendor they had. In Genesis 3, God curses the exile and prophesies his complete defeat and destruction (vv. 14, 15). Later, in the book of Job, Satan is pictured as roaming the earth, seemingly accountable to God for his activities.

Satan has fallen far. He wants revenge, yet he cannot attack the Holy One. So his next logical choice is to attack God's image.

We are the imagebearers of God. In counsel with his triune self, God chose to create humankind in God's likeness (Gen. 1:26, 27). God chose to crown this part of creation with the stamp of God's image, to bestow knowledge, righteousness, and holiness. Men and women were created with a stature and a relationship with God surpassing that which Satan enjoyed or could ever hope to attain. To add insult to injury, God has declared to us his unconditional love, a love that Satan apparently at one time enjoyed. So we can understand why Satan would want to attack us. Frustrated and angry, Satan knows God cannot be attacked—but God's children, God's imagebearers, are vulnerable. Satan's rage can be vented. Satan has found a target.

If you have children who are in some way attacked or in pain, you feel that pain yourself. Attacking us is Satan's way of attacking God. It is not so strange, then, that you, as a child of God, should experience the onslaught of the flaming arrows of the evil one.

A Question of God's Glory

Q. What is the chief and highest end of man?
A. Man's chief and highest end is to glorify God and fully to enjoy him
    forever.

—Westminster Larger Catechism, Q&A 1

For our salvation was a matter of concern to God in such a way that, not forgetful of himself, he kept his glory primarily in view, and therefore created the whole world for this end, that it might be a theater of his glory. (Geneva Consensus)

Children aren't the only ones full of "why" questions. God created us with knowledge. When that knowledge was tainted and substantially diminished by sin, "why" became a common part of our vocabulary and conversation, both with others and with God. Sometimes our questions are a way to challenge God; other times we ask out of pure frustration brought on by our inability to understand. I wonder how many times a day the question "Why, God?" is asked around the world. Or how often one person asks another, "Why would God . . . ?" We often ask such questions when we are trying to understand the existence of evil. We know, of course, that God cannot be blamed for evil that is ultimately the result of sin and Satan's direct or indirect involvement. But we wonder why God allows such evil to continue. We believe God is sovereign and that Satan can be struck down by "one little Word" ("A Mighty Fortress Is Our

God," stanza 3). Then why hasn't that Word put an end to Satan? What is God waiting for?

I believe it is a question of God's glory. Somehow God's name is and will be further glorified by allowing evil to run its course. Scripture abounds with testimony to God's glory. God's glory is so central to the purpose of creation and to our purpose that we must consider it a major factor in any discussion or study of theology, Christology, ecclesiology, soteriology, or eschatology. Creation declares God's glory. God's people are called to worship God, to sing God's praise, to give God glory.

> The heavens declare the glory of God; the skies proclaim the work of his hands. Day after day they pour forth speech; night after night they display knowledge. There is no speech or language where their voice is not heard. (Ps. 19:1-3)

> Praise the LORD. Praise God in his sanctuary; praise him in his mighty heavens. Praise him for his acts of power; praise him for his surpassing greatness. Praise him with the sounding of the trumpet, praise him with the harp and lyre, praise him with tambourine and dancing, praise him with the strings and flute, praise him with the clash of cymbals, praise him with resounding cymbals. Let everything that has breath praise the LORD. Praise the LORD. (Ps. 150)

In Christ's high-priestly prayer in John 17, we see that God's glory is a central theme. Christ's earthly ministry was coming to an end. The result would be that Christ himself would be glorified. The purpose of that glory and the very purpose in the completion of Christ's ministry was that the Father would receive glory:

> Jesus . . . prayed: "Father, the time has come. Glorify your Son, that your Son may glorify you. . . . I have brought you glory on earth by completing the work you gave me to do. (17:1, 4)

Paul makes it clear that this is also our purpose. Whatever we find ourselves doing, we should do it for the glory of God (1 Cor. 10:31). When Paul speaks to the issue of predestination, he is thinking way beyond our salvation. He is relating the details of God's plan for us to the glory that God receives when that plan is fulfilled.

> For he chose us in him before the creation of the world to be holy and blameless in his sight. In love he predestined us to be adopted as his sons through Jesus Christ, in accordance with his pleasure and will—to the praise of his glorious grace, which he has freely given us in the One he loves. . . . In him we were also chosen, having been

predestined according to the plan of him who works out everything in conformity with the purpose of his will, in order that we, who were the first to hope in Christ, might be for the praise of his glory. (Eph. 1:4-6, 11, 12)

Scripture abounds with instructions and descriptions that call us to glorify God. These include our own trials and sufferings (1 Pet. 1:7) and may even extend to the manner in which we die (note what John said about Peter's death in John 21:19). That we live for God's glory would be cause enough for Satan to attack us, but it gets worse (at least from Satan's perspective). We *share* in God's glory! Even though we have sinned and fallen short of God's glory (Rom. 3:23), we are told:

Now if we are children, then we are heirs—heirs of God and co-heirs with Christ, if indeed we share in his sufferings *in order that we may also share in his glory. . . .* What if he did this to make the riches of his glory known to the objects of his mercy, *whom he prepared in advance for glory.* (Rom. 8:17; 9:23)

He called you to this through our gospel, *that you might share in the glory of our Lord Jesus Christ.* (2 Thess. 2:14)

And when the Chief Shepherd appears, *you will receive the crown of glory* that will never fade away. . . . And the God of all grace, *who called you to his eternal glory* in Christ, after you have suffered a little while, will himself restore you and make you strong, firm and steadfast. (1 Pet. 5:4, 10) (italics mine)

We need to make sure we're grasping the intensity and depth of Satan's frustration. This is why he prowls around like a roaring lion. This is why he wants to sift us (Luke 22:31) and devour us (1 Pet. 5:8). Like the king of Babylon, Satan had said in his heart, "I will ascend to heaven; I will raise my throne above the stars of God; I will sit enthroned on the mount of assembly, on the utmost heights of the sacred mountain. I will ascend above the tops of the clouds; I will make myself like the Most High" (Isa. 14:13, 14). He risked it all to claim God's glory for himself. Not only did he not secure that glory; he lost what glory he had. Not only was he banished from the mount of God; God has chosen to share his glory with the likes of you and me!

Satan will do anything to prevent us from giving glory to God. He will sow seeds of unbelief. He will cause us to be angry with God. He will try to force us to compromise God's sovereignty in our lives. He will lie to us. He will bring discouragement. He will tempt us toward other pastures. He will play mind games with us and, when necessary and allowed, will cause us physical harm. And one of his most effective tricks is to instill in us a secular worldview that tries to explain it all away. Ravi Zacharias compares this secularizing influence to the disease of leprosy, slowly numbing us to the spiritual realities and dangers that confront us on a daily basis. But if we remain true and faithful in the battle, God, not Satan, will receive the glory.

John Calvin places this warfare in proper perspective: "One thing which ought to animate us to perpetual contest with the devil is, that he is everywhere called both our adversary and the adversary of God. For if the glory of God is dear to us, as it ought to be, we ought to struggle with all our might against him who aims at the extinction of that glory" (*Institutes*, I, XIV, 15).

In the next chapter we'll examine Satan's limits in this warfare. And we'll look at some theological matters and terms that are often misunderstood.

From *Apocolypse,* St. Michael evicting Lucifer from Heaven　　　　　—Albrecht Dürer, 1471-1528

CHAPTER 5

SATAN'S LIMITS IN THE BATTLE

In the last chapter we asked why Satan would bother to attack Christians. The answer focused on Satan's feelings of frustration and his desire for vengeance. Another way to answer the question is to focus on what Satan gains by attacking us. In this chapter we'll look at that issue and at the limits God has placed on our enemy.

First, though, let's take a look at biblical examples of believers being attacked by Satan. I am using several examples that are more thoroughly described in Fred Dickason's book, *Demon Possession and the Christian* (I will deal with the inaccuracy of the term "possession" later), which I would recommend if you're interested in an in-depth study.

One of the more obvious Old Testament examples of Satan attacking individuals is that of King Saul. We are told that the Spirit of the Lord left Saul and "an evil spirit from the Lord tormented him" (1 Sam. 16:14) and an "evil spirit from God came forcefully upon Saul" (1 Sam. 18:10). It would be difficult to deny that Saul was an Old Testament believer—he was anointed by God (1 Sam.10:1) and "the Spirit of God came upon him in power" (1 Sam. 10:10) as he prophesied with the other prophets. If we say that Saul was no longer a believer when the Spirit left him, we raise some serious theological difficulties regarding the place of faith in our salvation (whether Old Testament or New Testament faith); however, the fact that the Spirit left Saul does distinguish him from New Testament believers. God still recognized Saul as one of his own. This is different than God merely "using" an unbeliever for his purposes, as was the case with King Cyrus (2 Chr. 36:22). Saul's sinfulness caused God's blessing to be removed, but it did not necessarily alter his status as a believer.

Some will argue that this is an exceptional case because the Lord was the one directly involved in the sending of the evil spirits upon Saul. I believe that Matthew Henry's description of what happened is accurate: "The Devil, *by divine permission,* troubled and terrified Saul" *(italics mine).* Henry is simply recognizing God's ultimate sovereignty. The same type of recognition is given in 2 Samuel 24:1 for an event that we are elsewhere told was caused by Satan's hand: David's census of Israel (1 Chron. 21:1). While at first reading this might sound as though God were behind the evil intent of these spirits, we know from the broader biblical context that God is not the author of sin, nor does God cause or tempt people to sin. I believe that Saul was an Old Testament believer who came under the attack (albeit permitted by God) of evil spirits.

Perhaps the most familiar example of an Old Testament saint being tormented by Satan is that of Job. He was a believer, described as righteous (1:1), more than diligent in worship (1:5), and considered by God to be one of his own (1:8). Here again the attack required God's permission, but it was a direct attack by Satan himself on a believer.

A striking New Testament example is that of Ananias and Sapphira (Acts 5). When Ananias lies to Peter about the profit from the sale of his property, Peter bluntly asks, "Ananias, how is it that Satan has so filled your heart?" (5:3). It is as much a declaration as it is a question. Some argue that Ananias was not a believer, but nothing in the passages suggests that was the case. He and his wife are introduced immediately after the discussion of those "believers" (4:32) who "owned lands or houses and sold them," bringing the money to the apostles (4:34-35). Joseph is then mentioned as a good example of a believer who did this, and Ananias and Sapphira as bad examples (but believers just the same).

Another New Testament example is that of the woman whom Christ describes as "bound by Satan for eighteen long years" (Luke 13:10-16). In verse 16, Jesus clearly and purposefully identifies her as a "daughter of Abraham." It is doubtful that he used the term only to identify her as a Jew. Rather, he uses the term to identify her as a true believer, much the same way that the apostle Paul later identifies true children of Abraham (Rom. 9:8; Gal. 3:29). I don't know that Christ limited his healing only to believers, but surely some of the people among the crowds in the synagogues of Galilee from whom Jesus cast out demons must have been believers. There was faith present. It was the absence of faith that limited or caused Christ to limit his healing ministry (Matt. 13:58).

Despite these examples, Dickason is still careful to state that we cannot present conclusive biblical evidence (leaving no doubt) that Christians (believers) were demonized—that is, possessed by demons. For example, the Acts account does not precede the narrative of Ananias and Sapphira by saying "Ananias and Sapphira *were* Christians." However, we cannot ignore the fact that Satan has obvious motives for attacking believers; considering his goals, there is a certain logic in such attacks. We do have direct warnings and advice regarding Satan's attacks from Jesus himself, as well as from Peter, James, and John (his closest disciples), and from the apostle Paul. Given all this, it would seem that the burden of proof lies with those who would disclaim the possibility of demonic oppression against believers.

How Long Is Satan's Leash?

This brings us back to the limits God places on Satan. When we lived in Costa Rica, part of daily life was the reality of theft, especially in residential areas. All windows and doors had metal bars. Most houses had walls around the front and back yards, usually topped with barbed wire or shards of broken glass. Many people had the added protection of a guard dog—a Doberman or a German Shepherd the size of a small horse. It was not uncommon to be walking along at night next to someone's wall and feel your heart suddenly drop to the pit of your stomach as some colossal beast lunged just as you were passing the barred gate. Were it not for the gate, you would become a canine's late-night snack. The gate was the dog's boundary; it marked its realm of authority.

Satan is somewhat like a mad dog on a leash. He has his limits. His reach can go only so far. Part of Satan's reach is determined by what God, in his sovereignty, will allow in individual cases. Other limits are imposed by the reality that we are God's children. As discussed in chapter four, the implications of that fact are far-reaching.

To understand Satan's limits, we need to acknowledge that we are complex beings. We are far more than a natural, evolutionary by-product of chemical reactions resulting in our particular physiology. While there is little doubt that we are physical beings and what happens to us physically can affect us mentally and even spiritually, our wellness is much more than physiological wholeness and chemical balance. We think, rationalize, and make decisions. We feel and express emotions. We relate on a personal level, both to others and to God. We are spiritual beings with an innate need to be one in spirit with our Creator. All these aspects of our identity can be looked at individually, but we cannot separate out any one aspect and treat it independently of the others.

When healing is necessary, it must be holistic. Just as Paul uses the analogy of the necessity of the unified functioning of the body (1 Cor. 12), so healing needs to come to all parts (physical, mental, and spiritual) of the individual. If I trip and wrench my ankle, I may need treatment—perhaps a cast, some pain medication, and a few days of restrained use. That may be all it takes. However, if I were part of a mile-relay team scheduled to participate the following weekend in state finals, I'd be going through some real emotional trauma. If my sense of identity or self-worth were intricately tied to my success, my relationships with others and with God could be affected if my team lost the race. For example, I could become angry with God to the point that my fellowship with God would be threatened (though my relationship to God as his child would still be intact). This scenario is not so far-fetched; a simple misstep and twist of the ankle can have far-reaching effects!

Satan knows this and he knows us. He is aware and astute. He knows how, when, and where to strike in order to cause the most extensive damage to our ability to grow, bear fruit, and give glory to God. But we need to be careful here—I'm not asserting that "the devil made me do it" if I happen to trip and turn my ankle. But it's possible. While we want to avoid giving Satan undue credit, we need to be aware that he can and just might attack in a variety of ways. And while Satan may not actually trip us, he may take advantage of the fall by feeding our minds lies of negative self-worth. As we've seen, we could respond to these lies in ways that affect our mental and spiritual well-being. We need to keep reminding ourselves that Satan seeks his own glory. He will eventually expose his involvement, and we must be able to recognize him and to combat him when necessary. Being aware of his tactics and limits will help us when the time comes.

The illustration in Figure 9 has its own limitations. As with some of the previous diagrams, the simplicity of concentric circles drawn in two dimensions cannot do justice to the complexity of our holistic design. For example, the circles suggest a definite boundary between each area, but these areas, while distinct, overlap and interrelate. What happens to our bodies can affect our minds and spirits. Similarly, mental trauma can have a psychosomatic effect on the body. The darkened intrusion indicates Satan's ability and his limits. Let's look at some biblical examples.

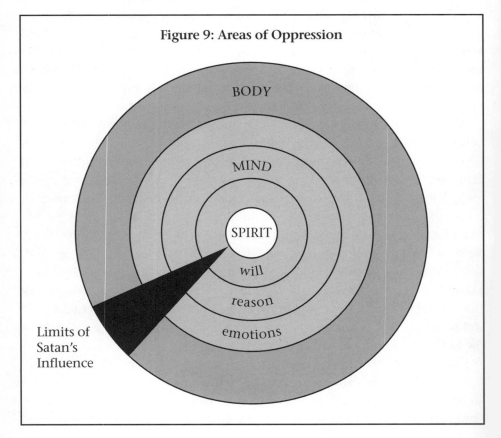

Figure 9: Areas of Oppression

BODY

MIND

SPIRIT

will

reason

emotions

Limits of
Satan's
Influence

In the last chapter we looked at the crippled woman whom Jesus healed in the synagogue. Clearly, this was a specific, physical attack by an evil spirit: "On a Sabbath Jesus was teaching in one of the synagogues, and a woman was there who had been crippled by a spirit for eighteen years. She was bent over and could not straighten up at all" (Luke 13:10-11). Or take the case of the "demon-possessed man who was blind and mute" (Matt. 12:22). Again, the attack seems focused on the body. It wasn't just a case of a demon-possessed man who happened to be blind and mute; rather, the possession caused the bodily difficulties. Note that Jesus healed the man by casting out a demon, which caused no little consternation among the Pharisees present (v. 24).

Perhaps the most familiar account of Jesus casting out one or more spirits is that of the Gerasene demoniac in Mark 5. Here it seems that the attack is more focused on the man's mental capacity, for we see a loss of volitional and rational control. This poor man was uncontrollably violent, so much so that he was forced to live among the tombs, where he would cry out and cut himself. But there was also a physical manifestation of demon possession, as demonstrated by his super-human strength, which allowed him to break loose from chains and leg irons (v. 4).

Another well-known account is that of the boy whom Christ encountered immediately after coming down from the Mount of Transfiguration (Matt. 17:14-18; Mark 9:14-27; Luke 9:37-42). In Matthew's account the boy is described as having seizures, yet Jesus casts out a demon (v. 18). It is interesting to note that Luke, a medical doctor, does not use the term for seizures but says that a "spirit seizes him" (v. 39). In Mark the demon is named by Jesus as "you deaf and mute spirit" (v. 25), but it also takes complete control over the boy's motor skills by throwing him into the fire or water in an attempt to kill him.

It has been suggested—perhaps because of a need to explain these events within a Western worldview—that these were cases of mental illness, or, in the case of the boy described above, a misdiagnosis of an epileptic seizure. In the absence of modern medical knowledge, things that people in Jesus' day did not understand were assigned supernatural explanations (the "God-of-the-gaps" theory). Allow me to point to two texts that seem to indicate otherwise:

> . . . and the people brought to [Jesus] all those who were ill with various diseases, those suffering severe pain, the demon-possessed, those having seizures, and paralyzed, and he healed them (Matt. 4:24).

> That evening after sunset, the people brought to [Jesus] all the sick *and* demon-possessed (Mark 1:32—italics mine).

In both cases, the writers distinguish quite clearly between those who were sick, diseased, paralyzed, or affected by seizures, and those who were demonized. Sometimes physical and mental conditions were caused by demonization, and Jesus took the appropriate action in rebuking or casting out the demons. In other cases physical conditions were simply that—physical conditions—and Jesus did not rebuke or cast out evil spirits to bring healing. While we don't know how many or what percentage of Jesus' healings dealt with demonic forces, we can safely assume it was significant. Along with healing the sick, dealing with the demonic was a major focus of Jesus' ministry of preaching the good news (announcing the kingdom of God).

We still haven't dealt with the center circle in Figure 9, the spirit. That's partially because it represents an area outside of Satan's reach. In my illustration of the turned ankle, I mentioned how various events in our lives can have a positive or negative effect on our spirituality. What I am referring to here, however, is our salvation, the one and only thing that brings us into spiritual relationship with God. It is this that defines us as Christians, children of God. This is something that Satan cannot touch. It is guaranteed. It is off-limits. While Satan's strategies may have a negative impact on our spirituality and reduce our effectiveness in accomplishing the purpose for which we were created—to glorify God—Satan cannot "kidnap" us from the loving arms of the heavenly Father.

The area of "spirit" in Figure 9 also represents the core of our being, in which resides God's Spirit, given to and living within every believer. This is why it is inappropriate to talk about a Christian being "possessed." The term indicates an ownership or control. That cannot happen to a believer because he or she is owned and in covenant relationship with God. The common translation of the Greek term *daimonizomenoi* would be far better translated as *demonized*—to have or be with a spirit or demon. There is no term in the Bible that is equivalent to "demon possession." Robert Unger defines demon possession as a state in which one or more evil spirits or demons inhabit and take complete control of their victim at will (Unger, *Demons in the World Today,* p. 102). When speaking of believers, Satan is limited to oppression; he cannot possess.

Degrees of Demonization

The main purpose in speaking about degrees of demonization is to show how Satan seeks to oppress, always working toward the goal of fuller control. Figure 10 is a modification of illustrations developed by Timothy Warner to help us visualize this concept.

When we talk about degrees of demonization, we want to be careful not to create rigid categories. The light vertical lines on the chart suggest that the lines between different levels of oppression are rather fluid. I want to avoid the tendency to diagnose the severity of one's oppression, which suggests different treatments for different levels of oppression. Nevertheless, it is important for us

Figure 10: Degrees of Demonization			
EXTERNAL INFLUENCE		INTERNAL INFLUENCE	
Temptations and Hassles	Habitual Behavior (Affects function)	Compulsive Behavior (Strongholds)	Demonic Control
Desire/Enticement	Corruption	Drive/Compulsion	Loss of control
Oppression	*Obsession*	*Inhabitation*	*Possession*
Christians and non-Christians		non-Christians only	
Responsibility of individual		Requires outside help	

to recognize that point at which we can no longer rely on our own resources to fight the oppression but must turn for help to the body of Christ.

While some authors spend much time discussing whether or not an evil spirit is attacking from the "outside" or residing on the "inside," this is not an issue I want to explore, nor am I sure this concept is helpful to obtaining release or healing. I do feel, however, that there is some significance in knowing if a particular issue we are dealing with is external or internal. For example, temptations or a habit may be the result of external forces (the world) or internal considerations (a predisposition of the flesh, which tends to be more controlling). As we've mentioned before, even if the attack or oppression is not directly from Satan, the chances are good that Satan will use it for his benefit, if necessary. Also, we should realize that not all oppression is related to our own overt sin. Sometimes it is the result of something that has happened to us. A traumatic experience or abuse may become a stronghold for fear or bitterness. While both are internal, one may be passive (fear) and the other quite active (guarding bitterness).

Let's take a look at three levels of possible oppression or demonization that can affect Christians.

Desire/Enticement

We all deal with temptation. This *can be* a form of oppression. It usually arises very naturally from our fleshly desires. The result of yielding to temptation is shame and guilt. While not detracting from our worth in God's eyes, shame and guilt are very effective in detracting from our concept of self-worth and from our ability to honor God. So how do we resist temptation? Not by escaping from the world and living in a vacuum that's free of fleshly enticements. Unless we were to leave our minds behind, certain temptations would tag right along, no matter where we went to "escape." We resist temptation by learning to live obediently.

It's possible for Satan or assigned spirits to get directly involved in the temptation process. Christian leaders often talk about a sudden, unnatural temptation to sin sexually. Many of these men and women have made conscious decisions to obey God in this area; then out of nowhere they are assailed with opportunity and temptation. But the responsibility is still the individual's. Resistance builds resistance, but strategic planning also does wonders in foiling an enemy's attack. I know of several Christian leaders who never travel alone or stay in hotels alone because they have learned when and where Satan likes to attack and when they themselves are most susceptible.

Defilement/Obsession

When we repeatedly give in to sinful desire, harmful habits or obsessions are formed, and defilement can follow. Some synonyms of *defile* are *spoil, blemish, dishonor, profane,* and *violate.* Some common areas of defilement include: abuse, drinking, pornography, lying, cheating, stealing, worrying, overeating, overworking, perfectionism, and self-defeating thinking and behavior (roots of depression). I'm sure you can add others to the list.

The difference in degree of defilement is measured in ability to control. For a nonalcoholic, taking a drink may not lead to a habit or to defilement. For a recovering alcoholic, however, yielding to that same temptation could be devastating and could result in the loss of significant control.

At this level the function of the individual is affected. Someone may adjust his schedule so he can visit the adult bookstore on the way home from work. Someone else may lie to her spouse about a drinking habit she claims to have given up. Someone else may be doing substandard work because drugs are affecting his or her ability to concentrate.

Here again, individual believers have the responsibility to change behavior in their lives that defiles them or negatively affects their function or ability to grow and to glorify God. And here too Satan may become involved in order to reduce our effectiveness. Once more, we are called to recognize our position in Christ, our authority as believers, and to resist the Devil so that he will flee from us (James 4:7).

Drive/Compulsion

People who are driven are not in control—they are exhibiting obsessive-compulsive behavior. Though they have tried to break free of the damaging behavior, they find themselves powerless to do so. They feel trapped.

This kind of behavior may be the result of a progression from temptation to habit to being controlled (as in the case of drug use, for example). Sometimes counselors will look for and treat chemical causes for these behaviors. Sometimes they may look for something more internal, something caused by a past pattern of behavior or traumatic experiences that point to an underlying cause or explain triggers for compulsive behavior.

From a spiritual viewpoint, these experiences could be called *strongholds* and the behavioral patterns referred to as *bondages*. This implies direct or indirect spiritual attack. Sometimes counselors call this kind of control *inhabitation*, because a spirit has claimed some "legal ground." This legal ground or stronghold has allowed a spirit to entrench itself in a person's life. Sometimes the individual is unaware of the stronghold or its origin. Sometimes, while aware, he or she may be so strongly oppressed that resistance seems impossible.

Again, we must not jump to the conclusion that all obsessive-compulsive behavior is caused by demonic attack. If medical and psychological therapy are showing no signs of helping a person suffering from compulsive behavior, however, we would do well to look at spiritual causes. Addressing spiritual causes, or even checking for the possibility of spiritual causes, can be done in a very loving, upbuilding, risk-free manner. This is where the body of Christ can use certain counseling techniques to assist the individual under spiritual attack. As illustrated in Figure 9, physical, mental, and spiritual aspects of an individual are all part of a unified, created whole. We must always be careful to recognize their interrelatedness and to treat each facet accordingly.

Christians can be affected at these first three levels: desire, defilement, and drive. The next level of Satan's control, which I refer to as full-blown possession, cannot take place in a Christian's life, and I doubt that there is much hope in helping such a person find freedom unless he or she becomes a believer. It may well be that possessed individuals are so harassed that even their ability to respond to the claims of Christ are hindered. Christian friends may have to exercise authority on their behalf in order to break these types of bondages and strongholds and call for God's Spirit to overcome and minister.

In the next section we will discuss whether or not it is up to the church to proactively minister to those in her midst who are afflicted at these various levels of demonization.

REFLECTION ON CHAPTERS 4-5

This section is intended for individual reflection and/or group discussion.

Bible Study

Read Ephesians 1: 3-8, 11, 12

1. What does this passage say about who you are as a Christian? Group members may want to take turns simply completing this statement: I am . . .

2. Chapter 4 defines a Christian as "someone who—by faith and the grace of God—is pardoned, reconciled, and adopted by God." These truths about our identity are all beautifully affirmed in this passage. When you imagine yourself confronting a very powerful enemy, what about these three hallmarks of your Christian identity gives you confidence and boldness?

Read Psalm 19:1, 2; Romans 15:5-9; 1 Corinthians 10:31; John 17:1-4

3. What recurring theme do you see in all these passages? Who are the main players?

4. Thinking in terms of spiritual warfare, what things in your life could you do differently so as to bring greater glory to God?

Read Mark 5:1-17; Mark 9:14-29

5. These passages both describe Jesus casting out demons. How are the two instances alike? How are they different?

6. Using Figure 9 in chapter 5 (p. 68) for reference, what area(s) were being influenced by demonic oppression in these two cases?

General Discussion

1. What effect does the reality that you have been pardoned, reconciled, and adopted have on you and your Christian walk?

2. Jot down some reasons that Satan may have for attacking you personally. Reflect on what your list says about your effectiveness in giving glory to God.

3. Thinking of areas of influence in which you are vulnerable, jot down things you feel *might* be specific attacks (direct or indirect) by Satan. How do you typically deal with such attacks?

4. How might you determine if any inappropriate desires, defilement, or drives in your life (see figure 10) involve spiritual attack?

5. If we indeed determine that something in our life might involve a spiritual attack, what could we do to end the oppression?

A Prayer

Lead us not into temptation
but deliver us from the evil one . . .

By ourselves we are too weak
to hold our own even for a moment.

And our sworn enemies—
the devil, the world, and our own flesh—
never stop attacking us.

And so, Lord,
uphold us and make us strong
    with the strength of your Holy Spirit,
so that we may not go down to defeat
    in this spiritual struggle,
but may firmly resist our enemies
    until we finally win the complete victory.

—*Heidelberg Catechism*, Answer 127

QUESTION 3

Should the church involve itself in spiritual warfare?

Good and Evil (detail of good)   —Victor Orsel, 1795-1850

CHAPTER 6

ENTERING THE BATTLE

As we think about the question that this section addresses—*Should the church involve itself in spiritual warfare?*—I am tempted to say "Yes, of course!" and leave it at that. But it's not that simple. There are questions that need to be answered, concerns that need to be addressed. And there is the issue of fear. Are real dangers involved in waging spiritual warfare? Does spiritual warfare involve a special calling, giftedness, and training? Are there alternatives to the church's involvement?

As I look at the notes in front of me, there is one that demands attention because it is scrawled in large capital letters—FOCUS ON CHRIST, NOT ON SATAN! It is so easy to lose our focus in a ministry of this nature. We tend to focus on the spectacular or the extreme. As I've said before, we can quickly lose balance, falsely identifying demonic activity in every setback and in every blocked goal (especially ministry-related goals!). We shouldn't give Satan undue credit; in fact, we shouldn't give him *any* credit. If and when Satan does attack, we turn toward Jesus. When we rebuke Satan or his forces, we do so in Jesus' name. When we resist the devil, we do so in the authority of the risen and glorified Lord. When we come against the demonic world, we must force it to look at Christ.

In this type of ministry, which often has dramatic results unachievable through other efforts, people naturally tend to give glory to the vehicle of ministry. Unfortunately, these ministries have a natural propensity to receive that glory for themselves. We, as individuals and as the church, must avoid this at all costs. If we see ourselves as the victors, we rob God of glory. Christ alone has won the victory. We, the church, are his hands and feet, his loving arms of embrace, his kind word of compassion, his healing in brokenness, and, at times, his sword of triumph over the evil one. We represent Christ and Christ alone, not ourselves, not a particular church or ministry.

Who Will Go?

I am reminded of the divine question of Isaiah 6:8, "Whom shall I send? And who will go for us?" If demonic activity is real and if we can be attacked, then the next question is "What can be done about it, and who's going to do it?" Like a good commander who never commits his troops and equipment to battle without measuring the options available, we need to examine our options on the spiritual battlefield. Is the church the only entity willing and able to address this issue? No, it is not. Other options are out there. Some are reliable, some are questionable. All offer only a partial remedy.

One of those options is modern medicine. With a treasure trove of technology and a drawer full of drugs that benefit the body and mind, modern medicine, for the most part, is not prepared to deal with the spiritual side of wellness. Many physicians who are Christians can and do address spiritual concerns of their patients. Some accept the validity of miracles and will even pray with patients. They are open to supernatural intervention. Many in the medical community will not or cannot believe in spiritual involvement (let alone demonic influence). Others feel called to minister only within their area of giftedness and expertise—medicine.

But many physicians admit that they have seen "things" in their practices that they cannot explain. Recently our congregation prayed fervently for an infant born with a hole in her heart, along with other complications. The condition was confirmed through several tests, but the doctors were reluctant to perform the high-risk surgery needed for correction. Finally, after further tests, they decided to operate, and upon "opening her up" discovered that the hole was no longer there. When I tell this story, some of my listeners express amazement that the doctors could have made such a "mistake." However, the lead surgeon said that the disappearance of the hole was a "mystery" that he would never understand.

Another option for dealing with spiritual oppression is modern psychology, which, in many cases, has all but forgotten that our psyche refers to our inner person. That inner person cannot be fully treated apart from our spiritual being. I admire Christian psychologists and psychiatrists who actively attempt to integrate spiritual realities in their treatment. I am afraid, though, that those attempting to do so are few and far between. Too often I have spoken with those experiencing spiritual oppression whose therapists have told them that they need to put God in the background, that their problem is not spiritual in nature, that they should not confuse the issue with religion. These therapists fear (sometimes with good reason) that their patients will overly spiritualize their problems and not deal with the real issues that are causing their problems. Many mental health professionals work in environments that discourage or even prohibit including the spiritual element in a patient's treatment. Let me reiterate that psychology has proven very beneficial in bringing healing to brokenness, and I am grateful for Christians who have responded to this calling. But secular psychology alone cannot adequately deal with spiritual oppression; in fact, it often denies it.

So while we may make use of legitimate medicinal and psychiatric options, it seems that the church must be involved in spiritual warfare. It alone can adequately address the spiritual dimensions of human beings. Unfortunately, the church has either not believed in spiritual oppression or it has proven helpless in ministering to people experiencing varying levels of oppression. The power of Christ is preached but not practiced.

Consider one personal example. As I write this, I am working with a young woman who has twice attempted to leave Satanism. She has sought help from several churches but so far has been turned away. Some members she's confided in have reacted with unbelief, telling her that the only possible explanation for some of her symptoms is a severe mental disorder. Others have drawn back in fear, saying, "Please don't get us involved in this stuff!" Some have overspiritualized her difficulties, urging her to repent and believe, since these things couldn't be happening to a Christian. She senses a strong feeling of helplessness, of churches being outside of their comfort and experience zones and having no frame of reference from which to offer help.

Clearly, if the church is going to involve itself in spiritual warfare, it has a significant learning curve ahead. But is this what the church is called to do? In Luke 4, immediately after his own battle with spiritual oppression in the form of direct temptation from Satan, we find Christ returning to the region of Galilee to teach. He arrives one Saturday at the synagogue of his own home town, Nazareth, and is offered the honor of reading and expounding Scripture. He chooses the scroll of Isaiah, from which he reads:

> The Spirit of the Lord is on me, because he has anointed me to preach good news to the poor. He has sent me to proclaim freedom for the prisoners and recovery of sight for the blind, to release the oppressed, to proclaim the year of the Lord's favor. . . . Today this Scripture is fulfilled in your hearing. (Luke 4:18, 19, 21)

This text refers to the literal realities of broken-heartedness, imprisonment, blindness, and oppression. I believe that we are called to follow Christ's model of healing, proclaiming liberty, giving sight, and setting free. But we must not ignore the spiritual dimension of this ministry. People are broken from years of spiritual onslaught that has prevented them from knowing Christ and his joy. They may believe the truth of the gospel in their mind and readily acknowledge its validity for those around them, but they are unable to break through their own doubts and insecurities. To be bound by habitual or compulsive behavior that increasingly controls your life is no less real than being bound by the four walls of a prison cell or the limitations of a work camp. To be spiritually blinded to the truth of the gospel and the realities of the Christian life has a much greater impact than the limitations of physical blindness. To be harassed and badgered by voices and thoughts that constantly drive you against your will is a yoke of oppression not totally dissimilar to the reports of dictatorships, brain-washing, and persecution commonplace in much of the world today.

What If We Don't?

After Jesus washes his disciples' feet, he tells them (and us) to follow the example he has set. I believe Christ means to be inclusive here, that we should follow his example in all areas of ministry that he demonstrated to his disciples, including that of spiritual warfare. But what if we don't? What if we choose not to involve ourselves in spiritual warfare? Unless we have somehow obtained release from this aspect of Christ's ministry, then we risk the results of disobedience in the same way we do whenever we sin.

Why doesn't the church become actively involved in spiritual warfare? Some of us in the church do not really believe that the battle exists, at least not on a level that requires us to participate. Others of us are simply afraid to fight—we know Satan is a formidable enemy and we fear his power. Uncomfortable and unfamiliar with the terrain, we choose to retreat rather than engage.

Some of us in the church may choose not to be involved because we do not fully understand all the theological nuances. For Reformed believers, this is especially true. We have a history of sound scholarship, of making sure our theological ships are all lined up before moving into uncharted waters. We are extremely careful not to do something inappropriate or, worse yet, unbiblical.

In the early 1970s my denomination (the Christian Reformed Church of North America) was dealing with the issue of neocharismatic influence in its churches. This issue caused much serious discussion and even some division. The debate focused on the more "extraordinary" gifts of the Holy Spirit. Although cessationism (the belief that miracles, extraordinary gifts, and so on, had for the most part ended with the apostolic age, after the availability of the New Testament canon) had never been an official dogma of our church, many held it to be true. Our synod made a major statement by proclaiming that the extraordinary gifts were available and valid for the church today. The report included counsel to the churches to be wise and discerning, but decisions on how to relate to these issues were left up to local congregations. Many doors were opened that had long been shut.

Let's suppose a local church follows through on this decision and considers holding a healing service. However, some church members hold back, afraid that things might get out of control or unsure of all the theological implications or simply doubting that supernatural healing should be sought in this way. So the church decides not to hold the healing service. The worst that could happen to this church is that it might miss out on a blessing God may have given. While serious—at least, in my opinion—that is not life-threatening. However, if that same church should decide not to be involved in spiritual warfare or to ignore Satan for those same reasons—fear, lack of knowledge, or unbelief—the worst that could happen is that Satan would sift that church and its members. We know that he has already asked permission to do so and that Jesus considered this to be a serious threat (Luke 22:31-32).

The church needs to be involved in helping people find freedom! I mentioned in the introduction that I do not have all the answers, that this book was intended to be introductory. It is my hope that it will be a wake-up call for some and that it will lead to further study. Although encouraged by others, I put off writing this book for several years. I was looking for all the theological answers to questions that I knew would be asked. I too had a need to get all my theological bows tied before going "public." I realized, however, that I was coming up with more questions than answers. Nothing was getting written. Nothing was getting done. I am not suggesting that the church stop searching for theological correctness. I *am* calling for more churches—and especially church leaders—to come out of the classroom and get involved in hands-on, field-based study.

Specific Problems for the Church

Three specific areas are problematic for the church in confronting the issue of spiritual warfare. They are lack of belief, fear, and lack of prayer. We have already addressed the first two to some degree, so I'll treat them briefly here. But lack of prayer is a separate and serious problem.

For the most part, lack of belief can be traced back to our Western worldview. We are trained to trust in cognitive knowledge. The testing and proving of spiritual realities does not work well in our Western paradigm. Seldom does a shift from a Western worldview to a biblical worldview happen overnight. Why? Partially because we are not simply replacing one belief system with another; rather, we are maintaining both but making one (Western) subservient to the other (biblical). This takes adjustment.

We don't always practice what we profess, but we do practice what we believe. If something goes against what we have always been taught (either formally or informally), we cannot by sheer force of will decide to be convicted about it. The Holy Spirit convicts, but it is difficult for us to convict ourselves. I doubt that we can force ourselves to believe something. There are, however, steps that can be taken to bring about conviction.

The first step in overcoming our lack of belief is being open to new ideas. If we are honestly open to a change in thinking, even a dramatic change in thinking (always measuring it against Scripture), then truth will start to make sense where we missed it before simply because we were not willing to look.

We can also choose to take some spiritual risks. We can actively take steps we may not have taken before, such as praying in a specific manner or rebuking Satan and renouncing the bondage of a particular sin or behavior if we have any reason to believe a spiritual element is involved. We can also risk examining our thought patterns and choosing to do things differently than before and perhaps differently than those around us (I'm not talking about throwing away our medications or handling snakes). Jesus did not hide the fact that following him would lead us in a different direction than that in which the world was going. To take such ego-endangering risks requires that we step out in faith. Faith and action are mutually dependent upon each other. We cannot take action without the initial seed of faith (often beyond cognitive knowledge), and it is the taking of those steps that allows our faith to grow.

The second problem that the church faces is that of fear. Satan has tricked us into thinking that he is too much for us. Hollywood has helped this along. Movies that feature exorcisms and the occult can fascinate unbelievers with the power available to those who are willing to barter their eternal destiny. And the same movies can frighten believers who speak of knowing Christ but don't seem to know anything of his power. As a spiritual counselor, I've heard people express these Hollywood-driven fears. Some seriously think that entering spiritual warfare will make them spit up green slime! Such fears are unwarranted.

Obviously we need to be wise and careful. We need to respect the power that God has chosen to allow Satan to maintain. But we have been promised the victory. Satan will be crushed under our feet (Rom. 16:20). Greater is our commander in battle (Jesus) than the prince of the powers of the world (1 John 4:4). We are commanded to flee the love of money, youthful lusts, and temptation, but when it comes to Satan we are instructed to boldly resist; it is he who will flee from us (James 4:7). Without trying to be unduly lighthearted, we need to remember that our enemy the devil is like a roaring lion, seeking to devour us, but God has pulled his teeth. This is not to suggest that he cannot harm or do damage or that he should not be taken seriously. It is simply to say that we will win the battle. We have tremendous authority in the name of Christ. It is an authority at which demons will flee and to which Satan must bow.

The third problem facing the church in the area of spiritual warfare is lack of prayer. It is difficult to pray that God will convince you of something you do not now believe. Often, though, a simple halting prayer that gathers together what little faith we do possess can have dramatic results and can help our faith grow. Effective prayer is closely tied to our worldview. A biblical worldview introduces us to spiritual reality, which, in turn, produces expectation. It is so much more exciting to pray believing that God hears us and is going to do something than it is to pray with little expectation that an omnipotent God takes us seriously and is active in our lives.

God is moved by our prayers. God cannot be manipulated, but God has chosen to allow himself to be moved by our prayers. God has promised to respond when we pray in harmony with his will. On the other hand, unbelieving prayer gets very little response (unless God chooses to respond anyway just to knock our socks off and get through to a hardened heart!).

It has been my experience that praying for the revealing of strongholds and against those strongholds and the powers that are invested in them is almost always concurrent with God's will. Destroying Satan and his work and freeing believers to grow and produce fruit brings God glory. When we pray for God's kingdom to be realized and advanced we are really praying against Satan's kingdom. The gates of hell have been here on earth, but the church has been called to come against that kingdom, and those gates will not be able to resist (Matt. 16:18). This is no mere skirmish—this is serious battle.

When we pray *for* something, we also pray *against* other things. If we pray for God's kingdom, we pray against Satan's. When we pray for healing, we pray against any hold Satan or a spirit may have. When we pray for salvation, we pray against Satan's influence and the hooks he has in that person's life. By entering into the battle in this way we are not negating the power or influence of the Holy Spirit. We are merely obeying God's command and wielding the power and authority he has given us.

Most of our spiritual battle must be fought on our knees. It is said of World War II that the war in the European theater was really won at Normandy on D day, almost a full year before German surrender. Christ has won the definitive battle for us. D day for the church is history. But now we are involved in a vast "mopping-up" operation with an enemy who is still very dangerous. The church needs to form its strategy, to pour its vast resources into prayer, to continue to fight until the enemy surrenders at last. Prayer is foundational. It is hard and serious work. It is indispensable.

What About Exorcism?

There's a misconception about spiritual warfare that can cause the church and individual believers to back away from helping oppressed people find freedom from spiritual or demonic influence. Many people equate spiritual warfare with exorcism. The two are not the same, though the end results are similar: spiritual influences are forced to release control and leave.

The word *exorcize* means "to cast out." This is certainly descriptive of what Jesus did. However, when we think of exorcism we often associate it with the rite of the Roman Catholic Church, as popularized by Hollywood. In

Catholicism, exorcism *is* a rite, performed only by those holding the special office (trained and gifted) of exorcist. But individual spiritual warfare is not a rite. It is not reserved for the clergy or others deemed qualified. It is not a special calling or an ecclesiastical office, nor does it require special giftedness. All Christians have the authority and the responsibility to stand against Satan's attacks in their own lives and in the lives of fellow believers.

True, some believers may be called to more active involvement, and some may demonstrate special gifts such as discernment and prayer. This is no different than some Christians being called and gifted in evangelism. It doesn't release other believers from the responsibility to evangelize or pray as opportunity and need presents itself. In the same way we are all called to be soldiers in the spiritual battle that rages around us.

In the next section we will deal with the final question—"How?" We will look at some practical issues of defense (protecting ourselves from spiritual attack) and offense (dealing with the attack when it comes).

REFLECTION ON CHAPTER 6

This section is intended for individual reflection and/or group discussion.

Bible Study

Read Matthew 16:15-19

1. What was the rock on which Jesus told Peter that he would build his church? How strong and sure is that foundation?

2. What do you think the phrases "and the gates of Hades [Hell] will not overcome it [the church]" and "whatever you bind on earth will be bound in heaven, and whatever you loose on earth will be loosed in heaven" mean?

Read Luke 4:16-21

3. In what ways is the prophecy recorded in verses 18 and 19 being fulfilled either through your personal ministry or through the ministry of your church? In what other ways can it be fulfilled?

Read Ephesians 1:15-23; 2:6, 7

4. In Paul's obviously fervent prayer for the Ephesians, what was it that he so desired them to be aware of? How did he describe it?

5. How does the truth stated in 2:6 relate to Christ's authority and to our own ministry?

General Discussion

1. Without denying the validity of their respective sciences, what are some practical ways in which the spiritual dimension of healing can be integrated with modern medicine and psychology?

2. Of the three problems mentioned in chapter 6—fear, lack of understanding, unbelief—can you identify specific areas with which you and/or your church may be struggling? What might be done to help resolve these difficulties?

3. What criteria would you use to evaluate the prayer life of your church? Does the prayer life of your church present a significant challenge to Satan? If not, what initial steps might be taken toward improvement?

4. Reflect with the group about your personal prayer life. Does it represent a challenge to Satan? What difficulties, if any, do you encounter? What do you personally find helpful in developing and maintaining a strong prayer life?

A Reading

In this world, bent low under the weight of sin,
Christ gathers a new community.
Satan and his evil forces
seek whom they may confuse and swallow;
but Jesus builds his church,
his Spirit guides,
and grace abounds.

—*Our World Belongs to God: A Contemporary Testimony*, stanza 37

QUESTION 4

How?

Spiritual Freedom #2

—Peter Sickles, 1942, living

CHAPTER 7

FOCUSING ON FREEDOM

- "I saw my therapist last week, and he said that my mental illness seems to be in remission."

- "It's wonderful to be able to look in the mirror and not see fat and ugly but pretty and slender, to not constantly struggle with eating disorders and body image. It feels so good to be free."

- "This has been so awesome for us. Everybody needs to go through this [freedom]."

- "This has been a glorious day for her; it's hard to believe this could have happened."

These are statements from or about people who sought and found relief from spiritual oppression. All four cases involved some previous professional counseling; two involved years of therapy and prescription drug treatments. The first statement, with its comment about mental illness being "in remission," is something I'd not heard before; perhaps the therapist used those words to describe something he could otherwise not account for. The third statement is from a couple who had successfully dealt with some issues that were keeping their marriage from being everything they felt it could be. The last statement was made by a client's counselor who wanted to sit in on a "freedom" session involving her client. The counselor had tried for quite some time to get her client to deal with some of the same issues, but extreme fear and anxiety had prevented progress.

My wife and I recently met with a woman who had suffered years of horrendous abuse, both as a child and later as a married adult. She had been in therapy for a number of years and was seeing a psychologist twice weekly and a psychiatrist once a month. We talked with her for more than three hours. On her next visit to her psychologist, he remarked that she had made about three years of progress overnight.

I want to be careful with testimonials (though I could give many more) because they sound like a quick fix—the magic dream pill that heals all woes. Keep in mind that I'm talking about spiritual issues. This is not the practice of psychology, psychiatry, or medicine, although it should be integrated with these disciplines for complete healing (sometimes spiritual issues block the effectiveness of treatment by these disciplines). Keep in mind too that spiritual issues can have strong physical and emotional impact.

I'm not implying that spiritual counseling puts an end to all other therapy. Note that in the case of the client whose psychologist said she had made three years of progress overnight, I did not say that her therapy was completed. In fact, she still had many emotional scars and some ongoing issues that needed to be dealt with, along with continuing medical symptoms resulting from her abuse. I never counsel people to stop medications and/or treatment. Only once have I contradicted the advice of a counselor, and that was with the concurrence of the client, her husband, and her prayer partners who were present. The next day her psychologist said our treatment made "good sense." Fortunately he was a Christian, and he was open to the reality of the spiritual dimension of her healing process.

I hope that these few examples have excited you about the possibilities of this kind of ministry. In fact, I hope you're already thinking about how you and your church can get involved. Let me say two things: first, this kind of ministry is great. It's exciting. It can be very effective. And second, it's simple (though not simplistic), and it's natural (not organically, but spiritually). These final two chapters deal with the "how" of spiritual warfare. In this chapter, which can serve as something of a warning or caution, we'll talk on a personal, individual level. We'll look at the interaction between our three enemies: the flesh, the world, and Satan. We'll examine the need to maintain balance. And we'll talk about our personal responsibility to choose freedom over slavery.

Three Enemies

As we attempt to live a life that gives God glory and to grow in our relationship with the God who gives us strength, we will find that not everything in our lives supports those goals. In fact, we are constantly confronted by powerful enemies, some physical and psychological, and some spiritual.

The first enemy we need to deal with is that of our "flesh." Of course, we don't want to fall into the error of denying everything that has anything to do with our flesh and the physical world. We and the world around us make up God's creation, a creation God declared to be good. At the same time, we need to be aware that we are tainted. We need to face the "flesh"—that part of us that seems to be in a constant state of rebellion against God. That's what we're referring to when we call "the flesh" our enemy.

It's true, as Paul says, that we Christians are new creations—"the old has gone and the new has come" (2 Cor. 5:17). Yet we know that our old selves have not yet been annihilated. We still struggle with the sins of our fleshly nature. John goes so far as to call us liars if we deny that sin is still with us (1 John 1:8). Even though Paul tells us that the old is gone (in terms of having control over our salvation), he realized that we need to continue putting off that old self (flesh) with its deceitful desires (Eph. 4:22). Paul's own battle with his sinful nature leads him to declare himself a "wretched man" (Rom. 7:24) when he realizes how natural it is for his old nature to go contrary to what his new nature desires. Most of the temptations that we must deal with can be thought of in terms of hand-to-hand combat with the flesh.

Our second enemy is the world. The world feeds the first enemy, our flesh. Strategically, it's as though the flesh makes a frontal attack on our defenses; if that fails, then often "the world" rides to its support by attacking one of our flanks. The world operates according to a worldview and societal structure that is every day more and more formed and controlled by our fleshly desires. The world in which we live is the environment in which our attitudes and responses to life are developed. It is the battlefield for the war we wage with sin.

I have difficulty thinking of a single fleshly desire that the world doesn't openly promote. That's why Western society is being called post-Christian or, by some, pagan. If your battle of the flesh is with an addiction, the world will feed it. If it is with immorality, the world says it's acceptable. If your struggle is with image or self-worth, the world sets a standard that causes you to self-destruct. Not only that, we willingly invite the world into our homes on a daily basis! Just watch prime-time television for one night and see if the world it portrays is Christ-centered or desire-centered.

Our third and most powerful enemy is Satan and the rulers, authorities, and powers spoken of in Ephesians 6:12. Satan is obviously involved to some degree in our temptations of the flesh and in the worldly norms that assail us. But let me reiterate two things before we continue. First, we are not called to, or even offered the option of, simply escaping from the reality of the world in which we live and the temptations that this world regularly presents. Jesus clearly meant for us to stay in the world: "My prayer is not that you take them out of the world but that you protect them from the evil one" (John 17:15). Second, we cannot shirk our responsibility to resist temptation in all its forms and strengths. Sin is sin, and while Satan may be its author, we have the responsibility to resist, sometimes with the help of other members of the body.

If the frontal attack by our flesh and the flanking attack by the world fall short, then Satan himself may attack us from our rear guard, often where and when we are least prepared. I believe that such passages as Luke 22:31, Ephesians 6:12, and 1 Peter 5:8 refer to these attacks by Satan or by his rulers, authorities, and powers. Sometimes those attacks are subtle; at other times, they are overt. Remember, however, that Satan has limits in this warfare (see chapter 5). Remember too that Satan's quest for glory forces him to expose himself. It's not difficult to search him out.

Our Need for Balance

Heeding C. S. Lewis's advice not to allow ourselves to become terrorized by the reality of spiritual attack, we need to maintain balance. As I write, the world is caught in the wake of a string of terrorist bombings in northern Africa. These and similar acts of terrorism have paralyzed some people with fear. They refuse to travel or to use certain modes of public transportation because they have suddenly become aware that terrorists could attack them in their own backyard. Such a reaction is unbalanced and paranoid; it robs its victims of their freedom and chains them to fear and trembling. We aren't meant to live that way.

Neither should Christians live in constant fear of Satan and his demonic forces. To do so is to lose the freedom that we have in Christ. On the other hand, we ought not to pretend that Satan doesn't exist. That would be as foolish as a government totally ignoring the threat of terrorists and taking no precautions to counter their destructive plans. Yet we sometimes feel that if we just "don't bother" Satan, he won't bother us. Truth is, we can't help "bothering" Satan if we live a life that gives God glory. If we choose to avoid doing that, then Satan no longer has to bother with us!

We are called to resist the Devil, not to hunt for him. We are called to recognize the nature of the battle and to be prepared, having donned the appropriate armor. We are called to be ready. That doesn't mean embarking on a spiritual scavenger hunt in search of a demon behind every bush and under every rock. Some will be there, but we have better things to do for the kingdom than to spend our time and energy digging around in the muck looking for Satan.

At times, and with good cause, the clergy, mental health professionals, and medical doctors reject the possibility of demonic or spiritual intrusion into peoples' lives. Too often they have seen people give Satan undue credit for sickness, accidents, the mental scars of trauma, chemical imbalance, and plain old sinfulness, while they reject treatment that deals with the real issue. I've heard people blame Satan when they lose their car keys, even though they misplace their keys at least once a week. But because they've lost their keys when about to leave for a prayer meeting at church, they pin the blame on Satan. And when they finally get to the meeting (after finding their keys exactly where they left them), they spend ten minutes of the time set aside for prayer talking about what Satan did to their keys! Even if Satan were involved (and it is possible), it's no big deal (even a toddler has the ability to pick up a set of keys and scurry off with them). If you have good reason to believe that Satan is truly involved in this kind of situation, rebuke him with your God-given authority and get on with living your life in a way that glorifies God. Keep *balance!*

Choose Freedom

Instead of focusing on the way Satan limits us, we can choose to focus on the freedom we have in Christ. Freedom is God's desire for his children. When Jesus healed the woman who had been crippled by a spirit for eighteen years, he spoke of freedom, "Woman, you are set free from your infirmity" (Luke 13:12). When he talked about discipleship and knowing the truth, he spoke in terms of being set free (John 8:31, 32).

Paul also focuses on freedom. He describes conversion as being set free from sin and the bondage of the law (Rom. 6:18, 22; 8:2). He tells the Galatian believers that "It is for freedom that Christ has set us free. Stand firm, then, and do not let yourselves be burdened again by a yoke of slavery" (Gal. 5:1). These believers had chosen to go back into slavery; they were binding themselves up with the old chains of works and ceremony. What bothered Paul was not that they were in danger of losing their salvation but that they were giving up their freedom, freedom purchased and guaranteed with Christ's blood. Paul's charge to stand firm and not return to slavery indicates the Galatian believers had a choice. They had to make the conscious decision for freedom and take the action required to claim it. They did not have to win it; they had to opt to live in it.

Freedom isn't always free. Nor is freedom license. The freedom that Christ offers—and gives us the authority to claim—has its costs. There's another side to the coin:

- Live as free men, but do not use your freedom as a cover-up for evil; live as servants of God. (1 Pet. 2:16)

- You, my brothers, were called to be free. But do not use your freedom to indulge the sinful nature; rather, serve one another in love. (Gal. 5:13)

- You have been set free from sin and have become slaves to righteousness. . . . But now that you have been set free from sin and have become slaves to God, the benefit you reap leads to holiness, and the result is eternal life. (Rom. 6:18, 22)

Choosing freedom implies obedience. It implies resisting those desires that lead to defilement. In the parable of the talents, the person who was faithful in small matters was given authority over greater things. If we are not obedient in those smaller areas where we have clear control and choice, we will not be able to resist in the larger areas that Satan is seeking to control through spiritual influences. We all have choices to make. Every time we choose truth and the way of righteousness, we begin to break existing strongholds and build resistance against Satan's attacks.

Here's a personal example. My natural behavior behind the wheel of a car might not always be described as Christlike. For years I thought nothing of speeding, using the justification of "everyone else does it" and "as long as I don't get caught (which I never did), no problem." Then I became personally convicted about obeying the law (whether I agreed with it or not) and started trying my best to stay within the speed limit. Needless to say, I soon developed the reputation of being an "old fogey" driver. Passengers (Christians included) often coax me to go faster, using the same justification I had used before. For me the issue is no longer a matter of obeying the law or avoiding a ticket; it's a matter of staying within a boundary I've drawn. Even though I may agree that going a few miles over the limit is not a big thing, I also realize that if I can't be obedient in the small things, I will have less chance of doing so in the bigger things. Of course, people who know me well could object, "But Jeff, what about this or that area in your life?" And I would have to admit, "You're right, that needs work too." The issue isn't perfection; it is striving toward perfection. It is consciously applying the truth that we have toward righteous living. It is choosing freedom.

When my wife and I take people through what we refer to as "freedom appointments," we help them deal with spiritual attacks by asking them to identify areas in their lives that do not represent truth. Then we guide them to confess, repent of, and renounce incorrect behaviors and thought patterns. Sometimes the untruth that binds people is a result of their own actions and thoughts; sometimes it is the result of what has been done or told to them. But the focus always has to be on freedom that comes from truth. Acting on this truth is always a choice, though often not an easy choice. Desire can be very powerful, and when Satan steps in to supplement desire, the difficulty of the choice increases dramatically. To choose freedom, our desire for freedom (truth) must be greater than the enticement that binds us.

One of the areas of truth versus lies is that of false religious experience, such as dabbling in the occult, participation in a false sect or cult, New Age involvement, and so on. I once made a series of presentations about spiritual warfare at a Christian high school. After the first presentation, which was a basic introduction, a student approached me, bubbling over with praise and enthusiasm about the topic. The next day I spoke about the need to confess, repent of, and renounce false spiritual experiences, and I mentioned things that many students have dabbled in such as using a Ouija board, tarot cards,

Dungeons and Dragons, Bloody Mary, seances, levitation, and so forth. Afterwards, the same student approached me, this time very offended. She felt there was nothing wrong with some of these activities, which she was regularly involved in; furthermore, they never had a negative effect on her. She also told me that even her pastor had said not to worry about these things because "they weren't real, anyway." Rather than arguing with her, I suggested that she allow God to show her if they were okay or not.

"The next time you're in a situation where your friends are doing one of these things," I suggested, "you should ask God to intervene and prohibit it from working if it's wrong and against his will."

"I can't do that," she immediately said.

Thinking that she meant that it would be embarrassing for her to pray like that in front of her friends, I said, "You don't have to do it out loud, just pray silently."

"You don't understand," she said. "I can't. When I'm involved in something like that, I can't pray."

Apparently, when she was calling on another spiritual power, her fellowship with God was so blocked that she could not pray, either physically or mentally. Even knowing the cost, this young woman was unwilling to give up the power of her "spiritual" experiences. She had not yet recognized that she was bound and, therefore, did not focus on freedom.

As in conversion, the first step in appropriating freedom is recognizing bondage or sin. While God is sovereign, he has given us a free will, and that free will assumes responsibility on our part. Even though in the next chapter we will look at some "steps" to freedom, it is not a quick-fix formula. It begins with taking responsibility and making choices. I'm reminded of a classic line in the movie version of Victor Hugo's *The Hunchback of Notre Dame* in which Judge Claude Frollo cries out in despair, "It's not my fault that if in God's plan, he made the devil so much stronger than a man."

The simple truth is that the devil is not stronger than those who are in Christ. We've been given the armor of God to protect us, as well as a mighty weapon for offense: "the sword of the Spirit, which is the word of God" (Eph. 6:17). God's word is Truth, Jesus Christ is the word made flesh, and by his light we will overcome the darkness.

Figure 11 shows seven basic areas of falsehood in which Christians often find themselves spiritually attacked. Figure 12 shows the truths that contradict and destroy the power of those lies or sinful behavior. The fruit we bear is a positive sign of life, vitality, and growth. If we are not being nourished by truth, our growth will cease, we won't produce any fruit worthy of being harvested, and, ultimately, we will be unable to give glory to God. Freedom is the process of replacing the lie, in whatever form it has taken, with God's truth and will for us.

Think of it another way. "GIGO" is an old computer term, meaning "garbage in, garbage out." Getting rid of the garbage frees us by removing Satan's strongholds in our life and allows us to live in victory. Charles Kraft

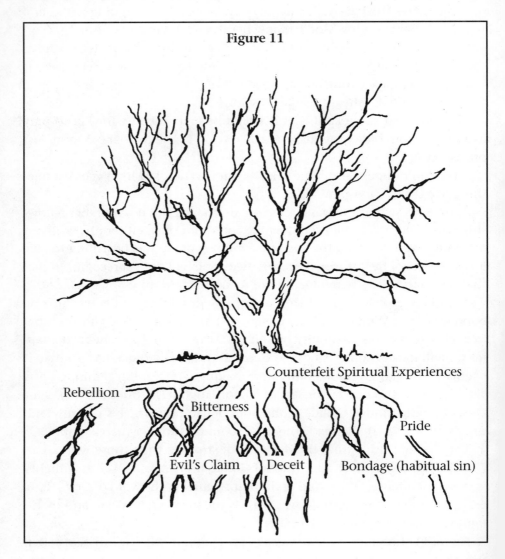

Figure 11

Counterfeit Spiritual Experiences

Rebellion

Bitterness

Pride

Evil's Claim   Deceit   Bondage (habitual sin)

says it memorably by pointing out that when you get rid of the garbage, the rats go away (Kraft, *Defeating Dark Angels*, p. 43).

In chapter eight we will go into further detail in each of the seven areas of truth as we discuss how to walk in victory.

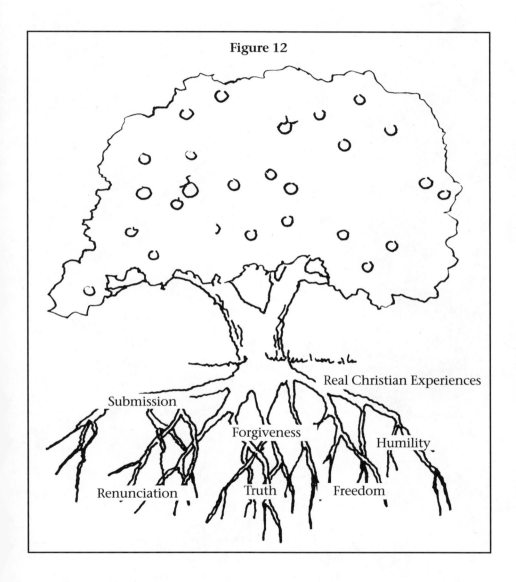

Figure 12

Real Christian Experiences

Submission

Forgiveness

Humility

Renunciation

Truth

Freedom

Healing

—Daniel Nevins, 1963, living

CHAPTER 8

WALKING IN VICTORY

A few years ago a local church decided to hire a new staff person in order to dedicate more time to the church's youth, many of whom came from "high-need" situations. Assuming her duties mid-summer, the new youth pastor wanted to get acquainted with the kids before the fall programs started, so she invited each one out for coffee or a soda. It wasn't long before she realized that a number of the young people did not want her around. They had nothing against her personally; they were upset because they felt that their youth program was going to be changed. Some voiced their dissatisfaction in no uncertain terms, even suggesting they would do whatever they could to sabotage her efforts.

In September, a youth-group retreat focused on the topic of identity. The new youth leader had each teen sit on a chair in the middle of a circle while his or her peers went around the circle reading aloud statements from God's Word that affirmed who they are in Christ (see Appendix A, "Who Am I in Christ?") The result was dramatic. Many kids were in tears; some were unable to sit through the reading. Afterward, many began sharing with the new youth pastor on a very deep and personal level. One teen turned over some drugs that he had brought along to the retreat.

Why the turnaround? Simply because this new youth pastor was meeting a very deep need. She was telling the kids that they were loved, that they were accepted, that they had intrinsic worth. The words weren't coming from their peers or parents—God was speaking to them through the Word. Once they began to see who they were from God's perspective, walls came down, strongholds began to crumble, and personal battles were won.

Freedom and walking in victory depend on knowing who we are in Jesus Christ.

Knowing Who We Are

Our churches are full of Christians, but many have never experienced the full life that comes from knowing who they are in Christ (John 10:10). Why? It may be because they can't get past the fact that they know themselves. They are keenly aware of their sin and are convinced in their hearts that a holy God cannot fully love and accept them.

In the children's fantasy *Quest for the King*, John White writes about Mary McNab, who loves Gaal (Christ), but is beside herself in hopelessness and despair. Why? Because Shagah, an evil sorcerer, has convinced her that she is cursed and that her past sins prevent her from having the relationship with Gaal that she once enjoyed. I think we have more than a few Mary McNabs in our churches. They identify themselves existentially, by what they do or have done, but not as children of God. They are trapped in a lie that they have told themselves and that Satan eagerly feeds. Unfortunately, the church, in its attempts to guard God's holiness and righteousness, has often unwittingly fueled the flames of self-incrimination, preventing those who have confessed their sin and who acknowledge Jesus Christ as their Savior from feeling forgiven and righteous, as God declares them to be.

Neil Anderson points out that even though we sin, nowhere does God identify his children as sinners. Despite our feelings of being unworthy, God identifies us as saints (Rom. 1:7; 2 Cor. 1:1; Eph. 1:1; Phil. 1:1) and as his children (John 1:12), with all the rights of children. Organizations such as Alcoholics Anonymous assist addicts by helping them to admit their addiction, a prerequisite to any hope of recovery. They are encouraged to wake up to each day facing the reality that "I am an addict." In many cases, however, Christians have outdone themselves in identifying their sinful condition. Thank God that we are not called to wake up every morning identifying ourselves by our sinful behavior! Rather, our identity lies in a far greater spiritual reality: *"I am a child of God, and I'm fighting a battle with sin (and sometimes demonic attack) in my life."* It's true that we must wake up to each new day ready to face the battle, but only with full recognition of who we are and who we belong to. We awake knowing that we are victorious in Christ.

Spiritual warfare, like any warfare, is fought strategically. Major battles aren't always won by the armies with the most soldiers and best weapons; they are often won by superior strategic thinking, by gaining the advantage. Gaining the advantage usually is a matter of position, and the best position to have in a battle is the high ground. If you look again at Figure 5 in chapter three, you will note that our position is on high ground—about as high as it gets—seated with Christ as the right hand of God. Not only are we loved, accepted, righteous, holy, and sharers of God's glory; we are also positioned with Jesus Christ, bearers of his authority, and recipients of the same power that came upon him when he walked this earth—the Holy Spirit.

Wielding Truth in Prayer

Even though theologian Paul Tillich comes from a distinctly different theological framework than we are assuming, John Maxwell recognizes the validity of one of his statements about the church and quotes Tillich:

The church is potentially a powerful body with a necessary arsenal at its disposal to change the moral character of this world. The fact that it is not doing so causes us to be painfully aware that its potential is not being realized . . . for while possessing the dynamite of the Gospel, the church has lost its detonator (explosiveness).

—As quoted by John Maxwell in *Partners in Prayer*, p. 95

I am not sure how Tillich defines that detonator, but Maxwell identifies it as prayer. He goes on to say, "When the people focus on God and give Him glory, He comes and makes the church a place of power. . . . churches have value because Jesus is in them" (*Partners in Prayer*, p. 97). What is true for the church is true for each individual Christian: prayer is a vehicle through which we are empowered by God's Spirit. It is a pathway to truth and discernment of God's Word and God's will, guiding us safely through spiritual (good and evil) reality. It is through prayer that God has chosen to allow his will to be bent. It has been said that Satan trembles when he sees the weakest Christian on his knees in prayer. I can think of no better approach to spiritual warfare and addressing demonic attack than prayer, combined with the light of God's Word.

David compares that Word of God to light, a light that illumines the path of God's way while exposing evil that lurks in dark corners. Jesus, the living Word, describes himself as the way, the truth, and the life (John 14:6). In the Word, then, we have the first piece of defensive armor that Paul mentions in Ephesians 6, which is truth (6:14). It is in this truth that we also encounter the rest of the pieces of the armor listed by the apostle: righteousness, the Gospel of peace, faith, and salvation. The Word is also the only offensive weapon mentioned, described as the sword of the Spirit (6:17). After listing our various pieces of protective armor and specifying our weapon, Paul then reminds us to pray (6:18).

In the prayers that he refers to as "Seven Steps to Freedom in Christ," Neil Anderson has provided a wonderful service to those struggling with an appropriate way to do battle against Satan (these steps are explained in detail in his book *The Bondage Breaker*). Anderson has taken the simplicity and power of prayer and combined it with the simplicity and power of truth. He uses prayer to state the truth of the Word (about who we are and who God is and, indirectly, who Satan isn't) and to request God to reveal truth about the battles and strongholds we face. He also uses prayer as the Spirit's sword, asking the Spirit to identify specific items, people, or activities that need to be repented of, renounced, or forgiven. The focus is not on Satan or an individual spirit; it is on God and the authority God has given to and through Jesus Christ.

The seven areas in which we need to seek freedom are shown in Figures 11 and 12 (see previous chapter): truth over deception; forgiveness over bitterness; submission over rebellion; humility over pride; freedom over bondage; and renunciation over acquiescence (compliance). Please see Appendix B for a specific prayer for each area. Note that the seven areas are broad and cover a wide range. Also note that each believer may not be struggling with all seven areas of oppression. Other areas—such as idolatry or materialism or fear—may also need to be addressed.

Perhaps to some this approach may sound like a canned formula for spiritual victory, akin to "three steps to marital bliss" or "ten steps to perfect parenting." Remember, however, that the prayers are intended to be a guide, nothing more. Often they are most effective when one is guided through the prayers by another trusted and mature Christian. And they are definitely not a one-time fix; in fact, I encourage pastor-led groups to go through the prayers on a regular basis. Think of this as a kind of spiritual maintenance, the spiritual equivalent of regularly changing the oil in your car's engine.

The seven prayers are in the tradition of the psalmist who requests God to search his heart for any offensive way and to create within him a pure heart. (Ps. 139:23, 24; 51:10). The intent of the seven prayers is to allow God to reveal any areas that could hinder fellowship or provide an opportunity for spiritual attack. Even if nothing of major import is discovered, the process provides an excellent time of preparation for the Lord's Supper.

While you will want to consult Dr. Anderson's writings for detailed backgrounds on the seven areas, allow me to offer a brief explanation of each, focusing a bit more on three of the areas that keep surfacing as major issues in counseling sessions.

Real over Counterfeit

This issue has become more apparent since the resurgence of New Age ideas. Except for its packaging and strong proselytizing efforts, nothing about the New Age philosophy is really new. People have long dabbled in various types of mysticism.

Many of the activities that represent counterfeit religious experiences fall into the genre of parlor games, such as table lifting and levitation, Ouija boards, seances, and so forth. It's quite possible that most folks involved in these activities don't take them seriously; they aren't convinced these games have anything to do with reality. Others dabble, recognize that there is some sort of spiritual power at work, get scared, and quit. The problem is that most of these "games" (along with a host of others) call upon spiritual power other than God. Whether or not the participants believe that other spiritual powers exist or whether they (the powers) respond is not the point. An invitation is made, at which point the participants open themselves up to spiritual influence.

Please don't misunderstand. I am certainly not saying that everyone who has ever dabbled in these or related activities has been or is being spiritually oppressed; however, the possibility exists, and that door of opportunity needs to be closed through confession and renunciation.

Another "counterfeit" category is that of divination, a sin that God places on the level of sorcery and witchcraft (Deut. 18:10) and condemns throughout the Old Testament. It is akin to idolatry because it seeks a source other than God for knowledge and truth. Activities of divination include Ouija boards, tarot cards, clairvoyance, astrology, and fortune-telling in its many forms.

Other counterfeit spiritual experiences include witchcraft, spiritism, the occult and Satanism, as well as involvement in cults, sects, and non-Christian religions. These all involve denial or rejection of truth; some involve, in varying degrees, volitional obligation to Satan. Just as all results of sinful activity are not eliminated by confession and pardon, so too some of the effects and strongholds ensuing from this involvement can linger until actively renounced and broken.

Maybe you're not sure if a certain activity you participated in was sinful or not. In that case, it's a simple matter to bring it honestly before God. One example of such an activity might be that of water-witching or dowsing, practiced on a regular basis by many missionaries in third-world countries. In this instance I would recommend a prayer along these lines: "Lord I confess that I have participated in dowsing. I am not sure if this is wrong in your eyes, but if it was and is contrary to your will and draws upon any power other than yourself, I renounce it in Christ's name and thank you for forgiving me and breaking any hold it may have in my life." It is a simple prayer that effectively covers the matter.

Truth over Deception

This area deals mainly with attitudes that do not concur with truth as revealed in God's Word. For example, we deceive ourselves if we are only hearers, not doers, of God's Word. We deceive ourselves if we think we can continue in our old sinful ways. We deceive ourselves if we think we can remain unaffected by associating with people engaged in openly ungodly activity. In dealing with this area, Neil Anderson also includes a section on doctrinal affirmation in which fundamental truths of Scripture are stated and claimed as truth.

This area is a key one for those who have dabbled with or been seriously involved in the occult, witchcraft, or Satanism. Often these people have experienced real spiritual power that they have not seen matched in average, mainstream Christianity. The lie embedded in their minds is that they cannot escape the hold that their activity has on them; they feel they "belong" to Satan or the spirit[s] involved in their counterfeit activity, and that nothing has the power or authority to overcome that evil spiritual influence. It's not uncommon for such oppressed people to feel extreme fear and panic when they try to pray, read their Bible, or attend church.

The antidote is to recognize the authority that has been given to Jesus Christ over all rule, authority, power, and dominion (Eph. 1:21). Truth wins out over deception when we realize that we as believers are seated in a position of authority with Christ (Eph. 2:6).

Forgiveness over Bitterness

I want to be cautious about saying that any one of the areas we're discussing is more important than another. They all need to be dealt with if we are to experience full freedom and growth. However, I'm convinced that the area of unforgiveness or bitterness robs many (if not most) Christians of their freedom and provides a stronghold for spiritual attack. Psychologists and medical doctors have long warned about the negative emotional and physiological effects of repressed anger. The apostle Paul specifically singles out anger when warning against the possibility of giving the devil a foothold (stronghold) in our lives (Eph. 4:26, 27).

Anger and the harboring of bitterness are the antithesis of the unity that Christ desires so earnestly for his body, the church. Not only does bitterness distract us from our fellowship, it also robs us of joy. It represents ongoing disobedience that has a strong negative effect on our spirituality. If we harbor bitterness in our soul, we do not have the freedom to walk in unencumbered fellowship with Christ. This stronghold prevents positive witness to Christ; it prevents the individual from truly reflecting Christ; and, ultimately, it prevents God from being glorified through us.

I do know some individuals who feel that they have been completely freed of bitterness. Their slate is clean—there is no one against whom they continue to harbor personal, malicious thoughts (though this doesn't necessarily mean they are fully reconciled to everyone who has offended them). However, I do not know anyone who has never experienced the need to forgive, who has never tasted the acid of bitterness. For some, the season of bitterness is long, for others it's short-lived, depending on the nature of the offense. It may be far easier, for instance, to forgive someone who lies to us than to forgive an abusive and unrepentant parent. A person's temperament also has an impact on how long he or she carries a grudge. Some Christians have painfully learned the lessons of keeping short accounts. Others have a psychological need to hang on to bitterness as a constant reminder that they've been wronged or as a control mechanism over the perceived offender who is seeking forgiveness.

One thing is clear: many Christians are being eaten away with a bitterness that they are unable to discard. This stronghold prevents positive witness to Christ; it prevents us from truly reflecting Christ; and, ultimately, it prevents God from receiving the glory that is intended to be channeled through us. In many cases this lingering bitterness can be traced to a faulty understanding of what it means to "forgive" someone. Let me explain what I mean.

We have all heard it said that God remembers our sin no more; when God forgives, he forgets. A contemporary Christian song has God asking the question "What sin?" concerning sin that has been confessed and forgiven. While this accurately expresses God's attitude toward confessed and forgiven sin, I suggest that our omniscient God does not "forget" our sins but rather chooses not to bring them to mind. God has made a conscious decision not to bring up our sins and rub our noses in them. That's why Satan was totally ineffective in his accusations against the high priest Joshua (Zech. 3). God's forgiveness is an ongoing choice of continuous grace and mercy. Viewed this way, God's forgiveness is more than a mere, single act of forgetfulness.

In forgiveness, we are not asked to forget—how does one consciously decide to forget? The truth is that we will always remember some of the things done against us. We are scarred and even permanently damaged by some of these things. Forgiveness asks us to choose not to hold the offense against that person, to release our right and our desire for revenge. Forgiveness is a choice to give the whole matter to God.

Another common misunderstanding about forgiveness is that it means saying, "It's all right." We have learned to put on masks, to avoid confrontation, to say, "It's okay, don't worry about it," when it is not okay. It was not okay when the offense happened, it's not okay now, and it will never be okay. And if we wait to forgive until we feel better or until the hurt goes away, we may never forgive at all.

While the results of the offense may linger for years, the bondage of bitterness does not have to remain with us. Forgiveness is a conscious choice to accept the ongoing hurt but to release the bitterness to God. It is a choice to benefit us, not the offender. Allen Guelzo describes forgiveness as "willingly throwing away our resentment at being wronged. This entails not just containing or restraining our resentment, but letting go of it entirely so we can be truly free of its influence." It is letting God be God and dealing with the offender as only God has the right to do.

Many issues of forgiveness relate to "forgiving" God for matters in which we feel God has failed us or been unfair. Obviously God does not need forgiveness because God does not sin, and we are in no position to forgive, even if God did sin. But we have declared that God is sovereign, and we therefore know that God could have caused certain things to happen or not to happen in our lives. At least, we ask, why couldn't God explain the whys and wherefores to us? When we realize we don't understand what God is doing in a particular situation, it's easy to become frustrated and bitter.

We should also keep in mind that forgiving someone doesn't mean passing judgment on him or her. One reason we find it so hard to mention the shortcomings of our parents is that we feel we are inappropriately judging them. In a Focus on the Family newsletter, Dr. James Dobson notes the difficulty of forgiving parents who have wronged us:

> Perhaps a mother rejected us instead of providing the love we needed. Maybe an alcoholic father was sexually abusive in the midnight hours. Little victims of such horror may still be consumed by resentment and anger many decades later.
>
> Psychologists and ministers now agree that there is only one cure for the cancer of bitterness. It is to forgive, which Dr. Archibald Hart defines as "giving up my right to hurt you for hurting me." Only when we find the emotional maturity to release those who have wronged us, whether they have repented or not, will the wounds finally start to heal.
>
> Jesus said it like this, "And when you stand praying, if you hold anything against anyone, forgive him, so that your Father in heaven may forgive you your sins" (Mark 11:25). Note that Jesus said nothing about who was right and who was wrong. Forgiveness, like love, must be unmerited and unconditional. Forgiveness begins the healing process.
>
> —From "Focus on the Family" newsletter, February, 1997.
> Used by permission of Focus on the Family.

As Dobson suggests, sometimes those who offend us do not repent. While the person primarily at fault needs to seek forgiveness to receive it, he or she may never do so. To hang on to our bitterness and allow it to develop into a potentially damaging stronghold while waiting for forgiveness to be requested is to choose to remain in bondage. It is to wait for something over which we have no control. But the fact is that we do have control over our choice to forgive. One young woman, after years of struggling for reconciliation, finally started walking in freedom after forgiving her offenders. This is what she later wrote about her experience:

I know that Christ preached a message of reconciliation, but reconciliation is bilateral; it takes two people. Forgiveness is unilateral. When I waited to offer forgiveness until repentance was present on the part of my offenders for my hurt and abuse, I was robbing myself of the freedom Christ gives me to choose to let go of my hatred and bitterness. While all my relationships have not been restored, I have been obedient to Christ's command to forgive, and I can move on. I am experiencing freedom because Christ is replacing my anger, hurt and bitterness with the peace, joy and love that he desires to share with me.

Despite such testimonies, some still question whether forgiveness should be granted before repentance takes place. Scripture, they say, points to a God who requires repentance. Are we expected to go beyond what even God would do? No, obviously not. We must bear in mind, however, that God's forgiveness is salvific in nature, resulting in eternal salvation. Human forgiveness, on the other hand, is not. We are not called to, nor could we, offer that kind of forgiveness. Our role in forgiveness is to deal with our hurt, our pain, our emotions, and give them to God for healing through the release of bitterness. If and when our forgiveness is requested by the offender, our role also includes grace and mercy.

Another concern is for abuse or violent-crime victims who have not been able to bring themselves to forgive a stubbornly unrepentant offender. Such persons may feel intense guilt for not being able to forgive, causing some even to doubt their personal salvation. We cannot and should not coerce victims into granting a false forgiveness; rather, we need to help them recognize the destructive consequences to themselves of holding on to bitterness and hate. Only by releasing bitterness and giving the matter over to God can healing begin to take place. We need to help these deeply-wounded people understand that they are not powerless, that the power to make the choice is theirs.

Asking for forgiveness (letting go of bitterness) is the third step in Anderson's "Seven Steps to Freedom" (see Appendix B). It's a simple process of prayer and self-examination, and requires a choice of will to complete. When you pray this prayer, you ask the Spirit to bring to mind persons who need your forgiveness, persons toward whom you may harbor conscious or subconscious feelings of bitterness. As God reveals such persons to your mind, you then offer a very specific prayer of forgiveness and release of each person and offense. As painful as the process of forgiveness can be, the outcome is overwhelming release.

I have lingered over the idea of forgiveness because it is so important to waging effective spiritual warfare. Forgiveness is absolutely crucial to inner healing. You cannot find freedom without it.

Submission over Rebellion

To a certain extent, rebellion is a normal part of everyday living. Pushing the limits is one of the ways we establish exactly where the boundaries are. But the kind of rebellion we're dealing with here is that of disobedience to God (think of Israel's frequent rebellion against God—see Psalm 78:56). Sometimes we express this with a raised fist to God; sometimes we vent our anger at those God has placed in authority over us: our parents, our employer, the government, and so forth.

I trust you are beginning to see how Anderson's seven steps are interrelated. I once counseled an individual who rebelled against any type of authority figure (she didn't realize this, but her friends could see it). Her rebelliousness, in part, stemmed from specific episodes of abusive behavior by her parents. Once she had dealt with this behavior through the forgiveness step, overcoming her rebellion was much easier. The next step was to confess her rebelliousness and to choose to leave it behind (repentance).

While these steps are voiced as prayers, they also serve as audible declarations to Satan that these areas are no longer footholds available to him or his minions.

Humility over Pride

"Pride goes before destruction, a haughty spirit before a fall" (Prov. 16:18). We are by nature proud. Western culture has long honored pride and the independent "do-it-yourself" spirit. Indeed, we measure our self-worth by personal achievement and by how we measure up in other people's eyes. This particular step, however, deals more with the sin of pride that places our self or our ability above God and others. It is the type of pride that says "I'd rather do my will than God's will." It is thinking that we are always right or that we are more important than others. It can even mean being proud of our humility.

My Reformed tradition places a premium on education. We've established a network of excellent Christian day schools and several outstanding liberal arts colleges. That's great, of course, but the risk is that we become too proud of our academic degrees. For example, I've seen good, capable persons passed up for church office simply because they're not college graduates. That's wrong. That's what pride can do.

The prayer in Appendix B asks God to help us recognize such attitudes of pride, confess them, renounce them, and choose to walk humbly with our God.

Freedom over Bondage

In a way this step becomes a catch-all for issues that have not been dealt with in the previous steps. It takes a look at habitual sin, which often takes people into the areas of defilement or obsession described in chapter 5 (figure 10). These kinds of sins typically include stealing, lying, outbursts of anger, lusting, gossiping, swearing, divisiveness, and many more. Sexual sin—including both sinning and being sinned against—frequently surfaces at this stage and can have a life-long impact. Persons I've counseled have often identified sexual sin as a foothold for spiritual oppression in their lives. Other areas of severe oppression or trauma may include homosexuality, abortion, suicidal tendencies, eating disorders, overwhelming fears, substance abuse, prejudice, and perfectionism.

To suggest that complete healing from all these oppressions always results from saying a short prayer of confession and renunciation would be misleading and inappropriate. However, I have seen such prayers break Satan's hold or his influence so that full healing becomes possible.

Renunciation over Acquiescence

This final step deals with the choice to actively oppose any spiritual power that may be influencing us. It pertains to spiritual influences that are beyond our control and that have nothing to do with our own sin or involvements. This step speaks to generational or ancestral sin—demonic oppression that continues through generational lines. Since many authors address this topic (see the bibliography at the end of this book), my comments will be brief.

Most of the authors who deal with this topic approach generational oppression as being the result of God's abandoning sinful men to their own lusts and depravity (Rom. 1:18-32). They also point to case studies that strongly suggest generational oppression. While we need to continue to do our theology on this question, we must take seriously the possibility of ancestral influence in our spiritual warfare. Acquiescence or compliance suggests passivity—doing nothing because it isn't "our problem" or sin. But it is our problem if it in any way prevents us from enjoying total freedom in any area of our spiritual life.

Another area of oppression that can affect us through no fault of our own is that of curses spoken against us. While this may sound bizarre, anyone who has dealt seriously with witchcraft or Satanism knows exactly what I am talking about. Curses are not just something we read about in fantasy literature; they are very real and very effective. Most Third World Christians coming out of cultures that were developed or continue to be steeped in animism will testify to the reality and power of curses. It is not at all unusual to hear of witches' covens or Satanic churches assigning curses against specific Christian leaders or ministries. We aren't always aware of a specific curse spoken against us, even though its results may be all too obvious. However, just as in all other areas of spiritual warfare, the power of any curse is dependent upon powers that must submit to the authority of Jesus' name.

The last prayer in the "seven steps" (see Appendix B) is directed at both known and "possible" generational oppression and curses. Just as David asked God to search his heart to see if there was any offensiveness (wickedness) and to correct it (Ps. 139:23, 24), so this step asks God to break the power of anything oppressing us of which we may not be aware.

Walking in Victory

Like anything else of value, our freedom must be protected and maintained. Spiritual warfare isn't a single battle; it is ongoing war. If you've decided to use the seven steps outlined above, you will find that you have established a significant beachhead from which to drive back opposing forces; however, you should not expect Satan to simply give up. Sometimes the attacks will intensify. Spiritual warfare is the art of choosing and utilizing the appropriate weapons against an identified enemy. This is not a quick-fix plan; it is a place to start. The victory is already ours; we must claim it and walk in it.

The seven steps and the prayers that go with them are tools, nothing more. Their power is in the truth they present, not in their structure or word choice. One woman who went through the prayers with my wife and me faithfully reread them, as necessary, to deal with Satan's continued attempts to regain lost territory. We had warned her that Satan would try to do this. One day she called me with more than a hint of panic in her voice because she could not find her written copy of these prayers. I simply asked her if she was depending on a magical formula or on the truth of God's Word. She was fine after that simple reminder.

Satan is like a mad dog behind a gate. Because God has not called us out of the world, there are times when we find ourselves on the wrong side of the gate. In that situation we should resist, not run. However, we can only do so with proper preparation. Along with wielding the truth, we must make sure that we are protected. That means staying away from situations that we know bring unnecessary temptation. We cannot play with sin. We have to learn to forgive. We have to learn to ask God each day to search our hearts and reveal our sin, then take that information before the throne of grace in confession. We have to learn to be quick to recognize improper thought patterns, then make them captive to Jesus Christ (2 Cor. 10:5). We have to learn to put on the full armor of God that Paul lays out in Ephesians 6 (see Mark Bubeck's *Overcoming the Adversary* for an excellent study of what this means).

Take a moment, if you will, to think back to the four questions that framed this book:

- Do Satan and demons exist, and are they active in the world today?
- Can Satan or demons attack Christians?
- Should the church involve itself in spiritual warfare?
- How?

I've attempted to show that Satan and his demonic forces are real and active elements in the world in which we live. While the church has never denied their existence, their activity has been questioned or ignored to the point of passivity. We need to submit all contemporary worldviews to a biblical worldview.

We've also noted that Satan's purposes and strategies remain basically the same, while allowing for cultural and contemporary adaptations. The biblical warnings to believers are clear—we can fully expect those who are actively fulfilling their mandate to glorify their Creator to come under the attack of the evil one.

Whether or not the church and individual Christians should be actively and offensively involved in spiritual warfare becomes a question of obedience. If we choose not to join the battle, it is highly unlikely that we will be effective soldiers of Christ. We have been promised that the gates of hell will not prevail (Matt 16:18); the very promise assumes an offensive against those gates.

How to do this? Certainly not brashly or carelessly. Rather, we are to wisely use our Christ-shared authority to announce the victory of truth and the truth of victory. Our task is not to re-stage battles nor to regain ground already won by Christ; it is to claim ground based on a victory already won. We must be bold, and we must be calm. We must not point to Satan and darkness but to Jesus Christ and light. Then the darkness must and will flee.

I could say much more, but this book is intended to be only an introduction to the topic of spiritual warfare. My hope is that it will encourage further study and growth. The appendices and bibliography give you some possibilities for immediate application, food for further thought, and suggested resources.

I am not in a position to make any prophesies about you personally, but I do know of your victory. So I encourage you, as Paul did Timothy, to fight the good fight and hold on to faith. Each day take care to strap on the armor God has given you. Take up your sword, the truth of God's Word, and in faith proclaim God's glory.

> Now to him who is able to do immeasurably more than all we ask or imagine, according to his power that is at work within us, to him be glory in the church and in Christ Jesus throughout all generations, for ever and ever! Amen.
>
> —Ephesians 3:20, 21

REFLECTION ON CHAPTERS 7-8

This section is intended for individual reflection and/or group discussion.

Bible Study

1. Read through the "Who Am I in Christ?" list in Appendix A. Read slowly and deliberately, remembering that each statement is a truth from God's Word that describes you personally. How does reading the list make you feel?

Read Ephesians 6:14-17

2. What are some practical ways to put on the pieces of armor and wield the sword of the Spirit as described in this passage?

General Discussion

1. Of the three enemies mentioned in chapter 7 (the flesh, the world, Satan), which represents the most obvious channel of attack in your life? Can you see ways that one enemy is supported by another? Once you've identified some lines of attack, jot them down and begin to think of effective counter-attack measures.

2. What, if any, activities have you or a personal acquaintance encountered that might qualify as counterfeit religious experiences? How can you tell if such an activity is indeed counterfeit?

3. How does it make you feel to know that if you are a Christian, God looks upon you as a saint?

4. Of the seven areas discussed in chapter 8, which one(s) do you think might represent potential areas of bondage or footholds in your life?

5. What "next steps" in spiritual warfare can you see yourself taking?

WHO AM I IN CHRIST?

Taken from *The Seven Steps to Freedom in Christ*, © 1996, Dr. Neil T. Anderson. All rights reserved. Used by permission. For further information, please contact Freedom in Christ (562-691-9128).

I Am Accepted

John 1:12	I am God's child.
John 15:15	I am Christ's friend.
Rom. 5:1	I have been justified.
1 Cor. 6:17	I am united with the Lord, and I am one spirit with Him.
1 Cor. 6:19, 20	I have been bought with a price. I belong to God.
1 Cor. 12:27	I am a member of Christ's body.
Eph. 1:1	I am a saint.
Eph. 1:5	I have been adopted as God's child.
Eph. 2:18	I have direct access to God through the Holy Spirit.
Col. 1:14	I have been redeemed and forgiven of all my sins.
Col. 2:10	I am complete in Christ.

I Am Secure

Rom. 8:1,2	I am free forever from condemnation.
Rom. 8:28	I am assured that all things work together for good.
Rom. 8:31-34	I am free from any condemning charges against me.
Rom. 8:35-39	I cannot be separated from the love of God.
2 Cor. 1:21, 22	I have been established, anointed, and sealed by God.
Phil. 1:6	I am confident that the good work that God has begun in me will be perfected.
Phil. 3:20	I am a citizen of heaven.
Col. 3:3	I am hidden with Christ in God.
2 Tim. 1:7	I have not been given a spirit of fear but of power, love, and a sound mind.
Heb. 4:16	I can find grace and mercy to help in time of need.
1 John 5:18	I am born of God and the evil one cannot touch me.

I Am Significant

Matt. 5:13, 14	I am the salt and light of the earth.
John 15:1, 5	I am a branch of the true vine, a channel of his life.

John 15:16	I have been chosen and appointed to bear fruit.
Acts 1:8	I am a personal witness of Christ.
1 Cor. 3:16	I am God's temple.
2 Cor. 5:17-21	I am a minister of reconciliation for God.
2 Cor. 6:1	I am God's coworker (1 Cor. 3:9).
Eph. 2:6	I am seated with Christ in the heavenly realm.
Eph. 2:10	I am God's workmanship.
Eph. 3:12	I may approach God with freedom and confidence.
Phil. 4:13	I can do all things through Christ who strengthens me.

APPENDIX B

SEVEN STEPS TO FREEDOM

The following prayers come from a booklet by Dr. Neil Anderson entitled *The Steps to Freedom in Christ.* In addition to these prayers, the booklet offers a full explanation of the teaching that corresponds to each step. It also includes the "Non-Christian Spiritual Experience Inventory," special prayers for specific problems, and recommendations for aftercare.

Opening Prayer

Dear Heavenly Father,

We acknowledge Your presence in this room and in our lives. You are the only omniscient (all knowing), omnipotent (all-powerful) and omnipresent (always present) God. We are dependent upon You, for apart from You we can do nothing. We stand in the truth that all authority in heaven and on earth has been given to the resurrected Christ, and because we are in Christ, we share that authority in order to make disciples and set captives free. We ask You to fill us with Your Holy Spirit and lead us into all truth. We pray for Your complete protection and ask for Your guidance. In Jesus' name. Amen.

Declaration

In the name and authority of the Lord Jesus Christ, we command Satan and all evil spirits to release (name) in order that (name) can be free to know and choose to do the will of God. As children of God seated with Christ in the heavenlies, we agree that every enemy of the Lord Jesus Christ be bound to silence. We say to Satan and all your evil workers that you cannot inflict any pain or in any way prevent God's will from being accomplished in (name's) life.

Step 1: Counterfeit vs. Real

Dear Heavenly Father,

I ask You to guard my heart and my mind and reveal to me any and all involvement I have had either knowingly or unknowingly with cultic or occult practices, false religions or false teachers. In Jesus' name, I pray. Amen.

Step 2: Deception vs. Truth

Dear Heavenly Father,

I know that You desire truth in the inner self and that facing this truth is the way of liberation (John 8:32). I acknowledge that I have been deceived by the father of lies (John 8:44) and that I have deceived myself (1 John 1:8). I pray in the name of the Lord Jesus Christ that You, Heavenly Father, will rebuke all deceiving spirits by virtue of the shed blood and resurrection of the Lord Jesus Christ. By faith I have received You into my life and I am now seated with Christ in the heavenlies (Eph. 2:6). I acknowledge that I have the responsibility and authority to resist the devil, and when I do, he will flee from me. I now ask the Holy Spirit to guide me into all truth (John 16:13). I ask you to "Search me, O God, and know my heart; try me and know my anxious thoughts; and see if there be any hurtful way in me, and lead me in the everlasting way" (Ps. 139:23-24). In Jesus' name, I pray. Amen.

Lord,

I agree that I have been deceived in the area of _____. Thank You for forgiving me. I commit myself to know and follow Your truth. Amen.

Step 3: Bitterness vs. Forgiveness

Dear Heavenly Father,

I thank You for the riches of your kindness, forbearance, and patience, knowing that Your kindness has led me to repentance (Rom. 2:4). I confess that I have not extended that same patience and kindness toward others who have offended me, but instead I have harbored bitterness and resentment. I pray that during this time of self-examination You would bring to my mind those people that I need to forgive in order that I may do so (Matt. 18:35). I ask this in the precious name of Jesus. Amen.

Lord,

I forgive (name the person) for (verbally share every hurt and pain the Lord brings to your mind and how it made you feel).

Lord,

I release all these people to You, and my right to seek revenge. I choose not to hold on to my bitterness and anger, and I ask You to heal my damaged emotions. In Jesus' name, I pray. Amen.

Step 4: Rebellion vs. Submission

Dear Heavenly Father,

You have said that rebellion is as the sin of witchcraft and insubordination is as iniquity and idolatry (1 Sam. 15:23). I know that in action and attitude I have sinned against You with a rebellious heart. Thank you for forgiving my rebellion, and I pray that by the shed blood of the Lord Jesus Christ all ground gained by evil spirits because of my rebelliousness will be canceled. I pray that You will shed light on all my ways that I may know the full extent of my rebelliousness. I now choose to adopt a submissive spirit and a servant's heart. In the name of Christ Jesus, my Lord. Amen.

Lord,

I agree I have been rebellious toward _____. I choose to be submissive and obedient to your Word. In Jesus' name. Amen.

Step 5: Pride vs. Humility

Dear Heavenly Father,

You have said that pride goes before destruction and an arrogant spirit before stumbling (Prov. 16:18). I confess that I have lived independently and have not denied myself, picked up my cross daily and followed You (Matt. 16:24). In so doing, I have given ground to the enemy in my life. I have believed that I could be successful and live victoriously by my strength and resources. I now confess that I have sinned against You by placing my will before Yours and by centering my life around myself instead of You. I now renounce the self-life and by so doing cancel all the ground that has been gained in my members by the enemies of the Lord Jesus Christ. I pray that You will guide me so that I will do nothing from selfishness or empty conceit, but with humility of mind I will regard others as more important than myself (Phil. 2:3). Enable me through love to serve others and in honor prefer others (Rom. 12:10). I ask this in the name of Christ Jesus, my Lord. Amen.

Lord,

I agree I have been prideful by _____. I choose to humble myself and place all my confidence in You. Amen.

Step 6: Bondage vs. Freedom

Dear Heavenly Father,

You have told us to put on the Lord Jesus Christ and make no provision for the flesh in regard to its lust (Rom. 13:14). I acknowledge that I have given in to fleshly lusts which wage war against my soul (1 Pet. 2:11). I thank You that in Christ my sins are forgiven, but I have transgressed Your holy law and given the enemy an opportunity to wage war in my physical body (Rom. 6:12-13; Eph. 4:27; James 4:1; 1 Pet. 5:8). I come before Your presence to acknowledge these sins and to seek Your cleansing (1 John 1:9) that I may be freed from the bondage of sin. I now ask You to reveal to my mind the ways that I have transgressed Your moral law and grieved the Holy Spirit. In Jesus' precious name, I pray. Amen.

Dear Heavenly Father,

I thank You that my sins are forgiven in Christ, but I have walked by the flesh and therefore sinned by _____. Thank You for cleansing me of all unrighteousness. I ask that You would enable me to walk by the Spirit and not carry out the desires of the flesh. In Jesus' name, I pray. Amen.

Lord,

I ask You to reveal to my mind every sexual use of my body as an instrument of unrighteousness. In Jesus' precious name, I pray. Amen.

Lord,

I renounce (name the specific misuse of your body) with (name the person) and ask You to break that bond.

Lord,

I renounce all these uses of my body as an instrument of unrighteousness and by so doing ask You to break all bondages Satan has brought into my life through that involvement. I confess my participation. I now present my body to You as a living sacrifice, holy and acceptable unto You, and I reserve the sexual use of my body only for marriage. I renounce the lie of Satan that my body is not clean, that it is dirty or in any way unacceptable as a result of my past sexual experiences. Lord, I thank You that You have totally cleansed and forgiven me, that You love and accept me unconditionally. Therefore, I can accept myself. And I choose to do so, to accept myself and my body as cleansed. In Jesus' name. Amen.

Step 7: Acquiescence vs. Renunciation

Dear Heavenly Father,

I thank You that I am a new creation in Christ. I desire to obey Your command to honor my mother and father, but I also acknowledge that my heritage has not been perfect. I ask you to reveal to my mind the sins and iniquities of my ancestors in order to confess, renounce and forsake them. In Jesus' name, I pray. Amen.

Declaration

I here and now reject and disown all the sins and iniquities of my ancestors, including (name them). As one who has been delivered from the power of darkness and translated into the kingdom of God's dear Son, I cancel out all demonic working that has been passed on to me from my ancestors. As one who has been crucified and raised with Jesus Christ and who sits with Him in heavenly places, I renounce all satanic assignments that are directed toward me and my ministry, and I cancel every curse that Satan and his workers have put on me. I announce to Satan and all his forces that Christ became a curse for me (Gal. 3:13) when He died for my sins on the cross. I reject any and every way in which Satan may claim ownership of me. I belong to the Lord Jesus Christ who purchased me with His own blood. I reject all other blood sacrifices whereby Satan may claim ownership of me. I declare myself to be eternally and completely signed over and committed to the Lord Jesus Christ. By the authority I have in Jesus Christ, I now command every familiar spirit and every enemy of the Lord Jesus Christ to leave my presence. I commit myself to my Heavenly Father to do His will from this day forward.

Closing Prayer

Dear Heavenly Father,

I come to You as Your child purchased by the blood of the Lord Jesus Christ. You are the Lord of the universe and the Lord of my life. I submit my body to You as an instrument of righteousness, a living sacrifice, that I may glorify You in my body. I now ask You to fill me with Your Holy Spirit. I commit myself to the renewing of my mind in order to prove that your will is good, perfect and acceptable for me. All this I do in the name and authority of the Lord Jesus Christ. Amen.

MENTAL-HEALTH CARE PERSPECTIVE

It should be obvious that the eight chapters of the text only touch the proverbial tip of a rather large iceberg called spiritual warfare. In fact, a careful and reflective reading of the text probably produced a number of questions and concerns. That's good—it's what reflective reading is supposed to do. Some of these questions may revolve around matters of theology—and clearly we need to be doing our theology as it relates to spiritual warfare. Other questions may revolve around our own life experiences.

My personal concern is that we don't neglect the emotional and psychological questions that arise. This concern grows out of the counseling approach that I've used to help others who are fighting serious battles against spiritual oppression. I am not trained in psychotherapy or pharmacology. I am aware of biochemical causes and the effects of trauma, but I am not in a position to give professional opinions on those matters. However, it's crucial that these disciplines not be ignored. The following dialogue represents part of a round-table discussion among several professionals involved in the mental health and counseling professions. I hope their comments raise additional questions for reflection as we seek to provide balance in all areas of bringing healing to God's children.

The participants were:

- James DeBoe, Ph.D., psychologist in private practice.

- Judith King, M.S.W., A.C.S.W., clinical social worker in private practice.

- D. Steven King, M.D., consulting psychiatrist in private practice.

- Nancy McGuire, M.D., former clinical professor of medicine, Grace Hospital Division of Wayne State University School of Medicine, currently in private practice.

- Joseph Rodriguez, M.S.W., B.C.D., clinical social worker in private practice.

- Richard Verkaik, M.C.E., M.Div., senior pastor, Friendship Chapel, Jenison, Michigan.

I (Jeff Stam) asked questions of the participants. I should mention that I was very pleased by the way the positions and advice of these professionals supported many of the points I tried to make in my book. None of the individuals involved in the round-table discussion had access to the manuscript—I wanted them to remain objective in this discussion.

Jeff Stam: What have been your experiences, if any, with spiritual oppression in the lives of your clients?

Nancy McGuire: My clinical practice is in infectious diseases and I see a number of patients who are impoverished and have histories of substance abuse—heroin and crack addictions, alcoholism, and so forth. Many of my patients have had problems in the areas of promiscuity and homosexuality. I also deal with a number of patients who have a terminal illness. I find that many of my patients have had severe devastating backgrounds and have been significantly oppressed. They are at the point of almost no hope in their lives. As a physician I feel that we are really not helping these patients. We are totally excluding the spiritual. [The spiritual] is not taught in medical school; I think we need to direct more of our time and our efforts as Christian doctors to this area.

D. Steven King: I'm thinking of someone who was referred to the hospital and came under my care. She was a beautiful young lady in her late teens, a very evangelical Christian. She came from a solid Christian family and had no sense of any abuse or neglect by her family. Her parents had been missionaries for a number of years. She was referred by a psychiatrist and a psychologist because of a depression they were not able to [successfully] treat on an outpatient basis. Both medication and good psychotherapy had been given. She came to our hospital, a textbook case of classical, major depression. She was suicidal, which is why hospitalization was being requested. The treatment was simply not working.

While I take a history, I listen with a third ear, so to speak. You have to listen as a professional, but you also try to listen with your spirit open to a different worldview. You try to get a complete history. In this case I found no family history of depression or outward reasons why she should be so depressed. She said that last summer she had gone back to Africa (where the family had been missionaries for eight or ten years) to work with a nurse who had been with the mission for a number of years. I asked when the depression started. She said it really began after she came home from Africa.

I asked if the nurse she was working with ever got involved in any spiritual difficulties.

"Oh yes," she said. "She was always having run-ins with the medicine man and the witch doctor; it was just an ongoing thing."

Immediately my antenna went up. I noted when this young lady's depression got started. I learned more about her life experiences. Later I asked her social worker if he thought there was something different about this case. "Yeah," he said. "I got a different feel when I was taking the family history."

Interestingly, within two or three sessions her primary therapist did a deliverance—I mean in the sense of focusing on a demonic force that had attached itself or done something while she was in Africa. Right in the therapy session, took authority over it, and this girl was transformed in a single session. I mean you could see that a clear and significant change had taken place. It was a wonderful experience, but it was very hard to convince some other professionals that such a thing had happened, including her Christian psychologist and psychiatrist who had made the referral. This girl was transformed and subsequently wrote a story about it. She is now in her thirties and has had no recurrence of any type of mental illness. She's married, has a family, and finished her education.

[It was a] textbook clinical depression, but she wasn't getting better with traditional therapy and medication and other things that are part of a proper, two-dimensional worldview treatment. A third dimension was necessary. That's one of my most dramatic cases.

Jeff Stam: Is that a general rule of thumb for you, that if normal means of treatment or therapy are having no effect, to start looking for the possibility of something spiritual?

D. Steven King: I think so. As a licensed professional, with malpractice and everything else that we have to deal with, my job is to look after the psychological, biological, and physical. That is what my area is. But yes, if for some reason we are doing everything right and not seeing any progress, then I will certainly, professionally, think maybe there is something more spiritual. The team that I used to have would pray at least every week, and we would pray for each patient. We would fast for some patients just to find out if there was another answer that our secular wisdom and knowledge wasn't providing. Sometimes we found it and sometimes we didn't. There are not easy answers to everything. In the case I mentioned, there was no biological or psychological route. There was a spiritual route that, I'm thankful, came to me and our team, and there was a great sense of healing and deliverance in her particular case.

Judith King: I have an example that is probably one of my most dramatic cases. This young professional woman from a neighboring city called for an appointment, feeling pretty desperate. She was a committed Christian, a Bible study leader in her church, a person who looked all-together, but she had been suffering from cruel, tormenting voices that would not leave. She'd also had about fifteen years of therapy from several different therapists.

When she came in to see me she was extremely agitated, could hardly sit still in her chair. She was frightened—terrorized, had been losing sleep because of this. Because she was being so constantly tormented with these destructive voices she had been sleeping with her Bible to overcome the "evil" she felt. She came into the office saying, "I need spiritual help." She was determined that what she was experiencing was a spiritual problem, and she asked if I could help her with that. She was familiar with Neil Anderson's material, and someone had recommended that she find a therapist who could take her through his *Seven Steps to Freedom.* She had visited her doctor the day before, however, and he had prescribed an anti-depressant medication, which she had taken for one day. I do believe in using psychotropic medications when appropriate, and I believe that as mental health professionals, we should use and be thankful for all available resources.

As I talked with her, in my mind I was doing an assessment wondering whether the voices were part of a psychosis or if the problem was spiritual (we have to do a good clinical assessment so we know what we're really looking at). She was desperate. "I just want to start these seven steps," she said. So we started into the first step. Within two hours she was 50 percent settled down—initially she had been so agitated and tormented that she was afraid to even leave the office. She was experiencing a safe place, and she was revealing things that she had never talked about in her life—and this to a perfect stranger.

The next day I saw her for another two-hour session. We completed going through the steps because this was definitely her agenda, and mine too as I saw the change in front of my own eyes. I saw her the next week and for several months following, and she reported that she was totally free from tormenting voices and the terror and agitation, free from all the symptoms, including the destructive thinking. She now felt empowered. She knew what she was fighting and had new, biblical tools to deal with the warfare that she was in.

Now, of course, she had started on the medication the day before the first time I saw her, and I didn't tell her to forego that, but I saw enough change in twenty-four hours to know that the medication was not what had caused the changes. I continue to follow up with her. There were definitely demonic forces that left. I experienced them myself in the office as they were bound and renounced. She was freed from demonic oppression through the power of God.

Jeff Stam: You mentioned follow up. Has she continued to maintain that level of freedom?

Judith King: Yes, she has, for over a year now. I did more therapy with her because there were other issues that came out that we had to go back and address. She has written that she is free and understands who she is in Christ, so that now she can take power in the name of Jesus to do spiritual warfare. That had been totally new to her. This was a woman who had gone through all the traditional approaches and had been asking for spiritual help for years and years. But the response was always sort of, "Well, tell me about your mother" or whatever. She was ready and wanting spiritual help, and she got it in the name of Christ.

Joseph Rodriguez: My first experience, in 1977, was not a good one. I was just out of graduate school. My first assignment was a twelve-bed unit dedicated for young people with psychotic disorders. There was a seventeen-year-old woman among the in-patient population. She had a Christian background. Her parents were in ministry. This young woman's family had no evidence of depression or other mental illness. Things were not going well for her. Medications were not helpful.

The first time I saw her I wanted to open our discussion with prayer. Having her permission, I simply asked Jesus to be present in the room and that her mind and heart be protected as we talked about the things that would be brought to her mind. I was not prepared for what immediately happened. Graduate school did not prepare me for this.

Sitting erect and wide-eyed, in a very rough voice she threatened to kill me. I was totally intimidated. I didn't know what to do or to say. Somewhat beside myself I said, "For Christ's sake, you are not!" I'm not entirely certain this was a proper prayer, being mostly an exclamation in reaction to being afraid. She rolled forward onto the floor with seizure activity, and all I could think to do was to call up a nurse to assess the young woman's health status. Physically she was fine.

Having no way to understand, I knew I had entered something completely out of my league. Within days her mental status deteriorated. The staff psychiatrist transferred her to a state hospital, thinking her condition would be chronic and in need of longer-term care. I lost track of her. I still wonder though; there was something about her that felt different. I wish I had known then what I know now. Would things have turned out differently?

Jeff Stam: What do you think you would do differently today?

Joseph Rodriguez: After being assured that she was physically okay, I would pursue the manifestation. I would see her again, assure her safety within the hospital setting, and begin asking her questions about her spiritual experience. I would take charge of the situation by dedicating the room and session to God's purpose. We would proceed in prayer for discernment, asking her to tell me the thoughts that came to mind as we prayed and talked. Usually anything tormenting her beyond the mental illness would reveal itself. We would go from there to a truth encounter. I feel a little smarter than the first time. I've had other experiences since but not that dramatic.

Richard Verkaik: I think my story is much like Joe's in the sense that you have to be spiritually tuned to what you're going to listen and look for. My education, even though it was theological, didn't prepare me to really listen to that side of people's lives. Only in the last couple of years have I been opened up to this. I've begun to read about it and to give it some credence.

As I look back in my pastoral care, I would now say that there have been many times I've had people in my office who were spiritually oppressed. But I wasn't looking for that particular problem. Today, however, it's an entirely different process because I'm asking different questions. I think that's the key—for people to begin to open up and to ask broader questions about a person's emotional state.

Jeff Stam: If I can jump ahead, Rich, on that one. How do you avoid, then, the accusation that you are merely finding what you are looking for? If we address counseling from a different paradigm, one that allows us to be looking for spiritual causes, are we going to automatically find spiritual causes?

Richard Verkaik: It's a matter of integrity. I think that if you go in to genuinely help a person, to be with a person, to care for a person, you have to trust the Spirit of God to reveal to your heart the reality of the situation. Go back to Joe's story—we say I would do "this" twenty years later, but if we're not looking for what we're really up against, we're not going to do anything different. I don't think that we can discuss this issue without having a segment of the theological or the mental health profession, or whatever it is, look at us with skepticism. But I think that those who go into a room with a person need to do so with complete integrity, and you've got to look at the whole scope of things, theologically, emotionally, from the past—whatever it is, and keep your mind open.

Judith King: To follow up on that, all of us in the caring professions, whether its mental health or pastoral care, want to help people. We look for psychological causes, and we try to do accurate assessments of psychological problems. We also look for physical problems, clinical depressions, anxiety diseases, and all of those kinds of things. But I think we're also challenged to look at the spiritual. That's the part that we haven't really been trained as well to look at.

To answer your question about the accusations, if we've done our homework and really looked at all the issues of a person's life and if a spiritual intervention has helped, then who's going to question that? I mean, if a person's better and they're free and they can function, then to me it doesn't matter about the accusations, because it's the person [that matters]. We're wanting to help people experience better health—mental, physical, emotional and spiritual. So, I think, to use a cliché, the proof is in the pudding. Is it working or not? If we've used integrity and have covered our bases, we can look at the accusations and say "so what."

Jeff Stam: Joe had mentioned earlier about his formal training not preparing him for this. Has your formal education in your respective fields inhibited you from being able to work with seriousness on the spiritual side of these issues?

Nancy McGuire: I think that there is a bias against Christian prayer or intervention in the setting of a hospital. You can do it a little more comfortably in an office setting. Also, today a lot of people are getting caught up in a lot of spirituality outside of Christ, and they're looking for answers. Most people have an emptiness and are looking for something to fill it. Basically, I believe that only Jesus Christ can fill that emptiness to make a person whole.

I went to a Roman Catholic university medical school and I really was not encouraged to become involved in questioning about this. Clinical medicine doesn't have all the answers. A number of patients do come into your office or the hospital with bodily complaints or their physical illnesses. That brings them in, but there is something much deeper that I don't think we as physicians are really taught about. I've learned to take spiritual histories on all my patients. If they're dealing with a major problem, I talk to all my patients this way. I feel that I can go ahead and start asking them questions about their beliefs in God. When I finish my evaluation, I ask them if it's okay to pray for them. A number of people have agreed to that, and I do follow up my patients, and I do see changes in those patients. Now, some of my colleagues probably think I'm crazy, but I think I'm doing what God has called me to do. I believe it's helping my patients, because I can't help them—only God can help them.

Joseph Rodriguez: My graduate education was biased. God was a factor to be neither reckoned with nor even recognized. My teachers genuinely wanted to help people and offered good insight. We learned about the psychological, biological, and social factors of human behavior, but none of the spiritual. I had a good education. I learned to help people. A number of people have come to me for help. Some improved, some got worse, and others stayed the same. Time and stress tested the good effects that were achieved. Those who I pointed toward Jesus eventually found answers that stood the test. Those who I helped realize their human potential eventually failed even when the counseling seemed successful.

People come to us hoping for answers. Jesus is the answer. Although a competent understanding of the human mind and emotion must not be minimized, Jesus in some way must touch the life with the truth. Unless we help people know their need for a touch from Jesus, they leave counseling as empty as they came, or worse if we fuel their confidence in self-sufficiency. Life in the world is rough, no match for false confidences.

Somebody must be recognizing this because more professional seminars borrow mystic practices to enhance the healing process. A strange hybrid of human potential and autonomous religion is spun in the service of self-sufficiency. Perhaps we ought not be surprised by the cultural turn toward the unseen, spiritual realm for answers. Any psychology without Jesus does not deliver.

Richard Verkaik: I wouldn't go as far as to say that there was a bias in my theological education. I was taught, obviously, that Satan distorted God's creation plan and that he is working hard to distort God's redemptive plan and all the theology that goes along with that. What I found out—again just in the last couple years—was that Jesus had a conversational relationship with Satan. By relationship, I mean that Jesus talked to Satan and confronted him. Jesus confronted Satan for what was going on around him and for what was going on in his own personal life and struggles. That's the piece that I possibly missed. For the first forty-some years of my life it was not a relevant piece of my own personal life or of my pastoral ministry. That has to be attended to. I think every pastor has to have a conversational relationship with Satan in a confrontational way.

James DeBoe: If I could add to that . . . In working and talking with a variety of pastors, and certainly with other psychologists, the notion that "Satan is a reality" is missing. We've all had the experience that if we start talking that way, we very quickly get feedback—from ministers as well as mental health professionals— that "you're way out on a limb."

D. Steven King: I think we've all had a pretty good formal education. Our education is just a reflection of our culture, but I don't think it's just an education problem. I trust that our universities turn out the best physicians, psychologists, social workers, and pastors, but our Western mind is being so secularized against the spirit and spiritual world that the universities and where we come from are just indicators of that. For years we taught psychiatry residents—including some wonderful Christian men and women. They wanted to learn about prayer and this and that, but I had to kind of hold them back—first they had to pass their boards and be credentialed. They had to learn to become excellent psychiatrists, psychologists, chaplains, or whatever. Then they could start to integrate the new knowledge that God gives. You may have to be a little bit adventuresome for that to happen.

Jeff Stam: Am I hearing you correctly, that the problem isn't with the education but probably with the paradigm in which the education is offered? That it is basically a scientific paradigm that does not encourage spiritual thinking?

D. Steven King: I think it's a two-dimensional paradigm, certainly at the university level. The secular worldview has crept into every part of education and every part of the church. Like Rich was saying—as a pastor for a number of years—he's had to change his paradigm from the good theological training that I'm sure he got from his seminary. It's our culture that we struggle against.

Judith King: Just to follow up on Nancy's comment, it seems that what's happening in our social-cultural context is that there is such a hunger to be met in the area of spiritual needs that there's a proliferation of endless ways to get in touch with the spiritual. So we end up with the whole New Age movement. People are hungry for something more, so there's a lot offered that is being masked as spirituality that is supposed to be helpful when it's really destructive. Already in my own graduate studies I had classes on Indian spirituality, and even though I felt like I had a good education, I remember at the time thinking "There's something about this that doesn't line up with my Christian beliefs." As Rich says, we need to confront that and its effects.

Joseph Rodriguez: It may be necessary to define spiritual warfare or spiritual counseling. For some, the concept conjures up a notion of an encounter of a "third kind," out of this world—something disconnected from what's happening to a person psychologically. Yet we hear more about the spiritual in secular seminars. A few years ago I went to a workshop on addiction. Throughout the presentation the leader kept referring to the spiritual aspect of her own recovery, but did not define it. Pressed to be specific about this, she described her "spiritual experience" . . . she was in turmoil one day and made a conscious decision to clean the house, a decision to go beyond her symptoms. She took out her vacuum cleaner and started cleaning, humming at the pitch of her vacuum cleaner's sound. A peaceful resonance came over her. This was the substance of her spirituality, the energy surrounding her and the environment. Spiritual warfare is neither out of this world nor is it a vacuum cleaner.

Nancy McGuire: More and more universities and medical schools are teaching this kind of stuff, for example, classes in alternative medicine. Medical students are learning this side of what I call "counterfeit spirituality." It's something that patients are looking for; they feel it gives them relief. Also, to back up, there are "doorways" that get patients into trouble—things like pornography or family problems. I feel that people have curses in their families, generational curses that they come across. I did not understand it—I thought it was mythology, but now I really believe that people are coming with spiritual baggage from generations ago. We really need to look into these things, to ask more questions about incest and such things. I used to just rush patients through, but now I take the time to learn more about who they are. I really believe that patients come to me not only for situations surrounding infectious diseases but also for spiritual problems. I really believe the Bible is my medical text in a way.

Jeff Stam: I think we need to be careful about definitions. When you say "doorways," Nancy, are you talking about strongholds?

Nancy McGuire: Yes, or what I believe the Bible refers to as footholds. I do believe that problems within the family, drugs, pornography, and so forth, open doorways or provide footholds. Another doorway is occult experiences. People get themselves into situations that they think are harmless.

Judith King: There are a number of people whose families are very definitely occultish. That's the family religion. So they bring a lot of spiritual oppression with them, almost as if it were intentionally put there.

I would also like to add that I've learned to think not so much "Is it one way or the other—is it psychological or spiritual, is it biological or spiritual?" I've learned that there is always a blend [of causes].

Often the human will has opened a door. I have talked with several ministers who have had deliverance ministries over decades; they've learned they really must work with the person and not just go in and "deliver." They work with the person and the choices that individual has made.

Jeff Stam: Let me jump then to the next question. In what ways, if any, have you tried to integrate spiritual healing or freedom in your practice, and what methods of integration have you found to be helpful? Also, have some ways proven to be unsuccessful?

Richard Verkaik: For years I've made a practice of praying for parishioners who would come in to seek counsel or just a listening ear. What has changed is that now I have begun to ask questions of certain people who I sense may be really dealing with more of an oppression. I listen to their stories—and they are very dramatic. I try to help oppressed people who cannot pray or who are just plain apathetic toward God. I see that as a real issue in my particular field. But I have begun to ask some questions about what they know and believe about Satan, where Satan is in their life. I am careful not to make it scary for them because I am very aware there's a whole segment of the community out there who hear "spiritual warfare" as a violent term. In a gentle way I have begun to ask penetrating questions to see where their perceptions are in the whole area of spiritual warfare. Often I have an opportunity to open up a whole new area of thinking for people, who, even though they have grown up in the church, have never thought of a personal devil who is trying, in one way or another, to destroy what they have. Whether it is their physical health, emotional peace, or relationships with other people, they never think of it. They do not put two and two together.

Jeff Stam: Depersonalizing evil seems to be an important issue, at least from a pastoral perspective. We talk about structures of evil in society, but we are not comfortable talking about a personal enemy out there. I hear you saying that we have to get back to recognizing Satan in our own personal lives.

Richard Verkaik: Yes, we do. And I'll go back to what I said before—that as part of the weaponry of living the Christian life, we need to teach our people to talk back to Satan in a conversational way.

Jeff Stam: Do you have any warnings about doing that?

Richard Verkaik: Yes. You know that this whole area frightens me as much as the next person. C. S. Lewis warned about two extremes—you can either take Satan too lightly or you can give him too much credit. I want to walk that middle road. I'm also afraid that people will see spiritual warfare as a shortcut to healing. You know, "Oh, this is Satan doing this? Well, let me go through this and God will take it away, . . ." when there are still issues out there. So I don't want to oversimplify this, but I do want to raise people's consciousness and awareness about spiritual warfare.

Judith King: I agree. We do not want to blame everything on the devil, but we need to find a balance here with personal responsibility. I have been trying to develop a model for traditional therapy using tools such as the *Seven Steps.* I've found that because these steps use a structured approach and the Word of God and the truth, I can cover a lot of material quickly, material that would take much longer with traditional therapy. The focus must be on who we are in Christ, empowering persons to take their own responsibility and to realize their own identity. The steps are a tool that they themselves can use to do spiritual warfare; and it's a lot less frightening because it is so Word- and identity-in-Christ based.

Jeff Stam: You've mentioned "less frightening" a couple of times. What are some of the risks that are involved in integrating spiritual warfare in a counseling ministry.

Judith King: Well, I've learned that not putting on the armor of God, not preparing ourselves, can lead to some backlashes. I have had some experiences, like you Joe, where someone all of sudden got a strange look on his face. When I asked him what he was thinking, he said that a voice just told him to kill me! So I started to sing, "Praise the name of Jesus, praise the name of Jesus!" Then, as my hair seemed to stand on end, I said, "Okay, I am a child of God, you are a child of God, where do you think that is coming from? Is that coming from God?"

Within seconds, the person said, "No, it's a lie, and I resist that lie in the name of Jesus." Then we were back on track again. Those are the kinds of things that seem frightening, but when you've been through a few of them, not really. You don't look for those kinds of experiences, but you know that you have authority as a believer in Christ.

Jeff Stam: How about potential risk to your clients, especially emotionally, when their balance or stability really isn't there and you integrate or mention the possibility of spiritual oppression or demonic attack. Is there risk there for the client?

Joseph Rodriguez: There are real practical risks. In the last few years, I have had the privilege of the Lord bringing me some of the most fragmented, damaged people I have ever met. Some of these people come with various levels of torment—those having fairly integrated personalities and others having severely fragmented personalities. A danger is not discerning when aspects of the personality are split up, when trauma or conflict-personified experiences make it seem as though someone else were there. If a well-intentioned helper tries to cast out the experience as if it were a demon, this is very dangerous. The tormented person is led into greater confusion and deception. Somehow very real parts of such persons and their experiences cannot come into Christ's presence for rescue and healing.

At the same time, however, there can be demonic activity, especially in people who were ritualistically traumatized. Spiritual discernment is crucial because there are times you cannot get a handle on what is wrong. The helper who does not realize dependency on the Holy Spirit is a dangerous person. Such a helper comes crashing into a very vulnerable and deceived situation. It is easy to become an instrument of Satan to drive the wounded further into deception and cause more harm.

Judith King: I believe that this is one of the advantages that we have as trained mental health professionals: that is, to understand the personality structure and to orchestrate, as we're taught to in therapy, to go with the client and to not push them too far, too fast. I've had some experiences where I've gone in too fast and the person has gone psychotic; their ego was too fragile to be able to take that. So I had to pull back and rebuild structure. Hopefully, as mental-health professionals or as trained counselors, we are able to assess that.

D. Steven King: I think the average professional would not rush in too quickly. They want to make use of the tools that they're most comfortable with, what their training has given and then add onto it. You asked about things that we've found helpful over the years. I first started getting interested in this in the late '70s, early '80s and I really found the inner-healing literature most helpful. It offered a logical, balanced way of putting the psychological and the spiritual—Christian spiritual—together to heal deep wounds and hurt that are inside most people, distorting our relationship with God, our intimacy, the needs that every person has. Integration should include inner healing and the whole idea of spiritual warfare that's normative for any Christian. Some people should also receive medical help for their biochemical needs. I also think that the gift of discernment that Joe talks about needs to be included. That's the only thing that I can trust. I've seen everything counterfeited as far as I'm concerned. The Bible says no word from God is void of power, and if you trust the voice of the Holy Spirit through discernment, there's a powerful intervention tool that God gives.

Jeff Stam: There's a certain paradigm assumed with that statement—the interaction and reality of the Holy Spirit and all that's involved in that.

Nancy McGuire: When I discuss these issues with my medical students and Christian colleagues, I try to get them involved in reading the gospel of Luke because Luke was a physician and basically documented very clearly what Jesus did in his ministry. I went through a personal experience with somebody from the pharmaceutical industry who was involved in witchcraft, and I started to understand the power of Satan and demonic presence as I learned about it. Then I started to see it more and more in clinical practice, not possession, but certainly oppression and demonization. I try to get my colleagues and students to understand the biblical worldview rather than just the view we are taught in medical school.

Jeff Stam: One more thing that I'd like to get a couple comments on: What kind of warnings would you put out and/or what kind of questions do you think need to be asked yet as we look at integration of the whole concept of spiritual warfare and counseling and medical healing?

Judith King: One warning is to keep our balance. We must not forget that Jesus Christ is our commander-in-chief. We must not become too demon-conscious and not enough Christ-conscious. Also, we have to be in relationship with other members of Christ's body, our fellow brothers and sisters, to help keep us on track.

Richard Verkaik: I would suggest that people who are just beginning to integrate the spiritual into their experiences take it slow. Sometimes something like this can be like a new toy. We take it out there and we begin to talk about it everywhere and we begin to apply it inappropriately, often because we simply don't understand it. As I said earlier, this has been a two-year movement for me. I now am really just beginning to integrate it into my pastoral work and even into teaching from the pulpit and my praying. It takes a while to feel comfortable with it, and I suggest people take it easy.

D. Steven King: Don't neglect getting a physical, a good check-up, and everything else that a physician recommends for your well-being. Don't be scared off by medications. The devil didn't give us medication; God gave us medication because he wants to relieve suffering.

Nancy McGuire: I would say to pray and to ask the Holy Spirit to be your teacher. He is going to guide in all truth.

James DeBoe: I would caution against being Lone Rangers. The people you're trying to help need people around them as they're going through changes. And you need people around you to just talk with and to team up with if you're doing this kind of work.

Joseph Rodriguez: Say to God, "Bring truth into my life; reveal within me any thoughts or imaginations that rise up against my knowing God." Ask God to reveal truth about your own life first, and give God permission to do anything he wants in your circumstances, in your life, to bring you to a full realization of who you are in Christ. God takes this prayer seriously. I would warn, however, to watch out when you pray this way—God will change you! It will cost you! It's a beautiful thing, but it can be painful. It brings you into that dependency, that humility, and that understanding that God loves you so much not just to take you to heaven, but also to leave you in a broken world to do what Jesus does.

ANNOTATED BIBLIOGRAPHY

Numerous resources are available on the topic of spiritual warfare. Unfortunately, not all are of equal value; some, in fact, are dangerously erroneous and misleading. And there is such a constant flow of new material being published that no one person can possibly read it all. So please don't assume that the absence of any resource from the brief list below implies a negative evaluation. Also, don't assume that I fully agree with everything said in the books I've recommended. The resources I've chosen present ideas and raise questions that deserve careful reflection and discussion.

Anderson, Neil T. *The Bondage Breaker.* Eugene, OR: Harvest House, 1990. 247 pages.

> The second of two books that detail Anderson's "Spiritual Conflicts and Biblical Counseling" seminar. Deals with a believer's authority over Satan, focusing on the counseling steps that are involved in guiding others through a process of freedom from Satanic or demonic influence. The book provides the basis for a "truth encounter" in which the counselee assumes responsibility for the removal of demonic influences (as opposed to a "power encounter" approach, which is more along the lines of an exorcism and the counselee is a passive participant). Concludes with seven "steps to freedom in Christ."

_____. *Steps to Freedom in Christ.* Gospel Light, 1996. 20 pages.

> This booklet offers a step-by step guide to help you resolve personal and spiritual conflicts, break free from bondage and renew your mind, and experience daily victory as a child of God. Please see Appendix B for excerpts and additional comments.

_____. *Victory over the Darkness.* Ventura, CA: Regal Books, 1990. 245 pages.

> First book and companion to *The Bondage Breaker* as part of the "Spiritual Conflicts and Biblical Counseling" seminar. The book focuses on the question of identity and recognition of who we are in Christ. This forms the foundation for the authority that the individual Christian has in spiritual warfare. Recommended as an excellent starting point for further reading.

Basham, Don. *Deliver Us from Evil.* Tarrytown, NY: Revell (Chosen Books), 1972. 223 pages.

> An interesting biographical sketch of a minister's growing involvement in spiritual warfare, even though the possibility of the existence of demons did not fit into his theology or twentieth-century worldview.

Bubeck, Mark I. *The Adversary*. Chicago: Moody Press, 1975. 160 pages.

> Excellent book for introducing the topic of spiritual warfare. Written from personal experiences, with several practical prayer tools. Recommended for beginning a more in-depth study on the topic of spiritual warfare.

_____. *Overcoming the Adversary*. Chicago: Moody Press, 1984. 139 pages.

> Follows up his first book, but from the perspective of ten more years of experience. A good biblical approach to Christian authority.

Dickason, C. Fred. *Demon Possession and the Christian*. Westchester, IL: Tyndale, 1987. 355 pages.

> The chair of the Department of Theology at Moody Bible Institute, Dickason gives a thorough treatment of the topic (not an introductory book). It is biblically grounded and offers a scholarly treatment of the highly debated question of whether or not a Christian can be demonized (he rejects the term "possession," even though it is in the title).

Evans, Tony. *The Battle Is the Lord's*. Chicago: Moody, 1998. 431 pages.

> In a very readable style, Evans deals with five basic areas: the theological question regarding the nature of spiritual warfare; the existence, purpose, and work of angels; Satan; the Christian's authority and its use; and spiritual warfare in the context of our personal lives, family, church, and community.

Kraft, Charles H. *Deep Wounds, Deep Healing*. Ann Arbor, MI: Servant Publications, 1993. 295 pages.

> Deals mainly with the issue of inner healing and touches many of the areas that are causes or sources of spiritual bondage. Also addresses the need and means for continued emotional healing.

_____. *Defeating Dark Angels*. Ann Arbor, MI: Servant Publications, 1992. 254 pages.

> Addressed to those with some experience in spiritual warfare, this book offers some in-depth treatment of key issues, yet is easy to read and uses many case studies. It begins with basic questions about the existence and power of demons, along with the believer's authority. It then goes into a technique that is a blend of a counseling, "truth encounter," and the more traditional "power encounter." The reader should be aware of the need to balance proper psychological expertise with some of the techniques offered, such as heavy use of visualization, "back-to-the-womb" experiences, and past memories.

Long, Zeb Bradford. *The Collapse of the Brass Heaven*. Grand Rapids, MI: Chosen Books (Baker), 1994. 267 pages.

> Written from a distinctly Reformed perspective, Long offers an excellent treatment on the question of worldview from a philosophical, biblical, and theological perspective. Recommended for in-depth study.

MacMillan, John A. *The Authority of the Believer.* Harrisburg, PA: Christian Publications, 1980. 96 pages.

> A classic reader, which is a compilation of two booklets: "The Authority of the Believer" and "The Authority of the Intercessor." It is concise and easy to read; however, its conciseness also leads to some rather dogmatic statements that are perhaps too strongly worded. Another good introductory source.

Miller, Calvin. *Disarming the Darkness: A Guide to Spiritual Warfare.* Grand Rapids, MI: Zondervan, 1998. 159 pages.

> A well-balanced, easy-reading treatment. Miller calls the reader to maintain balance and not to become overly dependent on non-biblical formulas or methodologies. He takes a serious look at some of the leading areas of demonic influence in our society.

Peretti, Frank E. *This Present Darkness.* Westchester, IL: Crossway Books, 1987. 376 pages.

> Extremely popular book written in novel form. It is not recommended as a "first book" on the topic. While it is very interesting reading, it includes many assumptions and very few explanations, due to its style as a novel. While it offers an excellent emphasis on prayer, it is fairly graphic and has had the tendency to frighten readers, another reason why it should be read after a different introduction to the topic.

_____. *Piercing the Darkness.* Westchester, IL: Crossway Books, 1989. 441 pages.

> A sequel to *This Present Darkness*. A very interesting commentary on some of the secular opposition the church faces in our society. Again, very graphic—keep in mind that it is a novel, not a case study.

Unger, Merrill F. *Demons in the World Today.* Wheaton: Tyndale, 1987. 209 pages.

> A well-balanced treatment that doesn't make some of the assumptions that other authors do, especially regarding initial belief in the demonic. Some of the biblical interpretation, however, is simply stated without providing defense or explanation, forcing the reader to have to assume the author is correct. Some of the data is outdated, going back to the first edition in 1971.

Wagner, Peter C. "The Prayer Warrior Series." Ventura, CA: Regal Books (Gospel Light), 1992-1996.

> Series of books on prayer as it relates to different levels and areas of spiritual warfare. While the books tend to deal with levels of spiritual warfare that go beyond that of personal oppression and into areas still hotly debated by many Christian scholars, they offer valuable insight to prayer on the intercessory level and its relation to broader, spiritual reality.

Warner, Timothy. *Spiritual Warfare.* Westchester, IL: Crossway Books, 1991. 160 pages.

> Provides a brief application of Scripture to the conflict between a purely scientific Western worldview and a biblical worldview and its application to spiritual warfare. Easy to read and recommended as an initial book in the study of this topic.

White, Thomas B. *The Believer's Guide to Spiritual Warfare.* Ann Arbor, MI: Servant Publications, 1990. 173 pages.

> Offers a practical tool for understanding different aspects of spiritual warfare, including advice on discernment of spiritual issues, prayers, and a number of case histories. Easy to ready and suitable for an introductory study of the topic.

_____. *Breaking Strongholds: How Spiritual Warfare Sets Captives Free.* Ann Arbor, MI: Servant Publications, 1993. 223 pages.

> Here White begins to deal more with specific prayer strategies and levels of spiritual warfare, such as identifying strongholds and coming against specific oppression against the church, cities, and other identifiable "territories." A little higher level of reading than *The Believer's Guide.*

Wright, Nigel. *The Satan Syndrome: Putting the Power of Darkness in Its Place.* Grand Rapids, MI: Zondervan, 1990. 198 pages.

> Wright deals with some philosophical questions in this good, general overview. Fairly easy to read but intended for a little deeper study of the question of evil.